# Damn The Statistics, I Have a Life to Live!

## Coping with a Brain Tumor
## My Personal Story

By

### H. Charles Wolf

ISBN: 1-4107-8623-4 (e-book)
ISBN: 1-4107-8622-6 (Paperback)

Library of Congress Control Number:  2003095634


This book is printed on acid free paper.


Printed in the United States of America
Bloomington, IN


1stBooks – rev. 08/22/03

# *Foreword*

When I was diagnosed with glioblastoma multiforme in June 2002, I did not have a lot of information about what to expect, except that it was a brain tumor in the left, frontal area of the brain. The basic information I got was that it was a high-grade (Grade IV) malignant tumor that was very aggressive. A glioblastoma multiforme is the most aggressive and fatal form of primary brain tumors. This tumor doubles every seven days if not controlled. The average life expectancy with glioblastoma multiforme is approximately one to two years.

There is more than just the battle against the tumor itself. I want to help people suffering from tumors to understand what the future holds and what special problems may occur. In my case, I could not speak for almost a week after surgery and I could not read at all for over a month. Not only do people have to deal with the tumor, but there are also the speech, memory, and cognitive problems that can be even more devastating than the tumor at times.

I've written this by putting in very personal feelings and information about my experience with the hope that it helps others with questions and maybe a better way to cope with their own battles. Being a project manager, I started a log the first day so that I could follow up on every aspect of my tumor. I also kept a journal to keep track of my own feelings and thoughts.

# *Dedication*

This book is dedicated to my family for their daily support as I fight the battle: my wife, Kathy, and my daughters, Amber, Charlotte, and Stephanie, who deal with this disease everyday. Without their daily encouragement and support, I would not be here. I also have to give credit to my 6-year-old granddaughter, Taylor, who has supported her Papa Charlie as he has lost his hair, eyebrows and suffered through other issues that are very difficult for a child. I also want to dedicate this to Adam, my grandson, who was recently born on May 2, 2003.

I want to thank my mother, Patricia; sisters, Sally, Pam, and Pattie; and my brother Rick for their tremendous and constant support.

I don't have the space to put all the friends, relatives, and co-workers that have provided the day-to-day support that keeps me going. But without their support, it would be impossible to deal with this. The e-mails, phone calls, lunches, and conversations are greatly appreciated.

I also need to thank Kathy, Amber, my mom and Kathy's parents for their editing assistance. Writing this book was great therapy. But with my continuing aphasia problems, I couldn't have done it without them.

And the people I cannot leave out are the doctors and especially the nurses. They are the ones that keep you going and make sure that things go well. I am especially appreciative of Swedish Medical Center and the Colorado Neurological Institute (CNI) Brain Tumor Program.

# *Table of Contents*

# Chapter
## 1

# The Day My
# World Changed

June 3, 2002 started just like any other day but turned out to be the day that changed my life forever. I showered, drove to work, and started my workday with my morning coffee. I was perfectly fine when I arrived at work that Monday. I had spent Friday and Saturday teaching a Project Management course for the company I worked for and had no problems. In fact, the program was well received and I enjoyed the great comments from the attendees.

I had several business trips scheduled over the next few weeks, including one to our office in Romania. Therefore, I prepared a list of tasks for my assistant to follow-up on during my travels. At 9:30 a.m., my assistant came into my office to review the list and to discuss how the Project Management course had gone. As I started to read the list to her she began to laugh and looked at me like I was messing with her. She added that I was not making much sense. We laughed and then I said I was looking at the sentences but could not read them. I felt like I was having a coffee buzz.

My assistant told me that she understood what I had written on the list and left. I didn't say much because I wasn't really sure what was happening to me. I went back to my computer to read my e-mail, and I saw there was a message on the computer's screensaver. I could see each word but I did not understand what the words meant. I was really getting scared now.

I called my wife, Kathy, and asked her if she was doing anything because I thought something was wrong with my brain. I don't know why I said that, but those were the words that came out. She worked for the same company and was able to come over very quickly. Kathy thought I was kidding and that I just wanted her to come over to my office for some reason, but she came over right away anyways. It was a good thing I called her right away because I would not have been able to contact her later by phone or even let people know what the problem was because I could not speak without talking gibberish a few minutes after Kathy arrived.

Kathy was in the building right next to mine and only took two minutes to arrive. By the time she arrived, I was worse. I had tunnel vision and things were getting dark. Kathy immediately knew something was wrong because my speech didn't make a lot of sense. She took me immediately to our truck to take me to the hospital. Littleton Hospital was only ten minutes away and we didn't think an ambulance was necessary. For anyone that may experience this in the future, I would suggest that an ambulance be called immediately.

My vision had started to narrow further and my speech was nothing but gibberish. At this time, it was not obvious what the problem was. As I sat in our truck while she went to get the keys, I panicked because I didn't know how to get out of the truck. I was so disoriented that I did not even understand I was in a truck.

At this point, I was terrified, I didn't know what was going on and my condition was deteriorating and becoming even worse. Kathy returned and we headed to the emergency room. I was trying to maintain consciousness to keep Kathy from becoming too upset but I was losing it quickly. At this point, I didn't know if I would be alive when we arrived. Still unaware of the problem, our fear was increasing as we drove.

**Trying to Write: I Think I Wanted My Wife to Call Someone**

When we arrived at the hospital, I ran inside, with Kathy right behind me. I remember trying to talk to the emergency room attendant. She could not understand what I was saying and I must have appeared really bad because she took me immediately to the emergency room without asking for my medical card, even though the waiting room was crowded. I was very thankful that the nurse acted immediately and Littleton Hospital took care of the serious people first. Kathy said they did not ask for the medical card until much later, after the CAT (Computerized Axial Tomography) scan.

While I was in the emergency room, I felt myself going into convulsions. I tried to maintain consciousness, but I blacked out. That's all I remembered until I woke up later that evening and found out that I had suffered a grand mal seizure. A grand mal seizure is the most severe kind of seizure involving a loss of consciousness and violent convulsions.

They gave me a CAT scan, an MRI (Magnetic Resonance Imaging) scan, and an MRA (Magnetic Resonance Angiography) to check out the brain for problems related to a stroke. I also received a spinal tap to check for infection, chest x-rays and probably some other tests that I don't remember. The doctors were trying to find out what the problem was, since I had been completely healthy and in great shape with no other sign of illness.

The neurologist came in Thursday night and brought in some pictures from all the scans and tests that had been done. The good news was that my entire body, except for my head, was in excellent condition. In fact, I have two arteries in one kidney. I didn't know if that was good or bad, but at the time it sounded good. The neurologist also said that the emergency room doctors had called him for treatment. They wanted to give me an anticoagulant stroke drug and he would not let them. He said that a stroke didn't make much sense since I was young, didn't smoke, and I was in such good shape. He said if they had given the anticoagulant to me, it probably would have killed me. I was lucky with doctors so far. I owe my life to the emergency room doctor and the neurologist, Dr. K. Ravilochan.

The MRI of my head showed a one-centimeter tumor, the size of an M&M®, in the left hemisphere, the speech and motor area, of my brain. It showed that half my brain had swelled because of the tumor and the swelling was causing the speech problem.

**"You have a brain tumor." That is one of the most terrifying things to ever hear.**

It was especially scary since my father had died from a brain tumor in 1995, which had metastasized from renal cancer. He only lived for a little over a month once his tumor was discovered, and never left the hospital. I soon learned it wasn't the same type of tumor my dad had, but it was still terrifying. I would have to get a neurosurgeon to tell me what type of tumor I had.

I immediately started to research brain tumors and what I may have to face. As I explored brain tumors there were several things that I thought were very important to do. First, I suggest you set up a logbook to record all your treatments and what the doctors say. This is very important, especially as your treatment progresses. Second, set up a journal where you can record your activities and comments. I found this very important to record my thoughts, ideas, or feelings as I battled my tumor. Third, set up an area to keep the information you've collected in an organized area and refer back to it often. Fourth, if you have children or others that are important to you, I suggest you start a book for each of them and write in it frequently. You may want to write ideas that you wish to share after you have passed away. This could be very important to people in the future. These would be even better if you survived and were then able to share with your family what you went through.

The first question I had, and the one that is asked of me most frequently, is how do you get a brain tumor and what is it. I have been unable to get a solid answer on what causes a brain tumor, but there is a lot more information on what a brain tumor is. Most sources describe a brain tumor as an abnormal mass of cells that are multiplying in your brain. I had no symptoms or any indication that I had a tumor until the day of my seizure.

Primary brain tumors behave differently than brain tumors caused by other cancers. They start in the brain and usually do not travel to other parts of the body. In a lot of cases, they even have their own blood supply. This is different than the type of tumor my father had. His tumor metastasized from his kidneys. A metastasized brain tumor is a secondary brain tumor that has started from a different part of the body, such as the kidney and traveled or metastasized to the brain.

I found out I had my tumor when I had a seizure and my speech became gibberish. Other ways that a tumor may be recognized are by: headaches, especially if the pressure seems to increase, falling, or paralysis, which is what happened when my father's tumor appeared. These are some of the things that may indicate a brain tumor. Unfortunately, by the time you recognize the symptoms, it usually has reached a point where you need to take some action because it has already caused some problems. The problems generally are a result of your brain swelling and not being able to escape your skull.

I know that I have a tumor, but what is next? How bad is it? And what do I do to cure it. The answer to a lot of these questions comes with the biopsy.

On June 6th, I had my first meeting with Dr. Timothy Fullagar, a neurosurgeon, who told me it was probably an astrocynoma or oligodendroglioma. He stated that tumors were rated from grade 1 to grade 4. I did not have a clue what that meant. I knew it wasn't good and I knew the grade was important. Dr. Fullagar told me that a needle biopsy is the best way to find out what type of tumor it is, as the method of treatment is dependent on the type and grade. I thought a needle biopsy just did what it said, that a small needle was inserted into your brain to take a sample. That was scary enough. But, I soon found out that the needle biopsy was huge and more complicated than

I thought! The biopsy was done by cutting the skin and then drilling a hole in the skull!

The doctors explained the Stereotactic surgical procedure. A frame would be placed on my head and more MRIs and CAT scans would be used to make a 3-D model to determine exactly where to go. A hole would be drilled into my skull and a needle biopsy would be performed. A hollow, narrow needle is inserted to collect a sample of the tumor for analysis. The biopsy was needed to get a sample of the tumor for analysis and to determine which type of tumor is present. The needle biopsy was scheduled for June 10th, but it would take three days to complete the analysis as to what type of tumor it was. This was the beginning of having to wait for news. The waiting was almost unbearable!

I had already started my logbook. I used a logbook to record everything that was going on. I guess as a project manager, I wanted to understand the situation and handle whatever comes up. I would recommend a logbook for any serious illness. It helps you keep track of what's going on and helps you to remember what has gone on. I guess I was getting ready for the most complicated and important project of my life!

I did not sleep at all waiting for the June 10th surgery day to arrive. I had spent all the time in between checking out tumors on the Internet. All the answers were not very good and some were totally unacceptable. This was one of the first times I was really forced to face my mortality and had no idea what would happen.

Since the doctor thought it might be an oligodendroglioma or astrocynoma, I focused on these areas. I didn't realize how many different types of brain tumors there were and how you treated them. Most pieces of information just stated that glioma tumors grow from glial cells – that helped! But then I found more information: glial cells are cells that form the supportive tissues of the brain. They rest between the nerve cells, and most brain tumors arise from the different types of glial cells.

An oligodendroglioma develops from glial cells called oligodendrocytes and usually occurs in young adults. An astrocynoma arises from glial cells called astrocytes. Both are primary brain tumors which means that they originate in the brain rather than spreading from cancer in another part of the body. The good news was that primary brain tumors don't spread to the rest of the body – if there is any good news with a brain tumor.

I started to get some of the tumors' grades and names. Using the World Health Organization (WHO) grading system, I looked up the potential grading. The grading system goes from Grade I to IV. Grade I tumors are the least malignant and are usually associated with long-term survival. Grade IV tumors are the most malignant type of tumor.

Reading through this information was very scary. Most of the information shows that only 1 to 2 % of the people survive for more than 2 years. That was not an acceptable answer for me.

We checked into Swedish Hospital at 5:00 a.m. on June 10, 2002. We filled out all the papers and then I was taken to have the pre-operation MRI. For the MRI, they added some gadolinium contrast to make the brain and any problems more visible. I also had a CAT scan of my chest to be sure that there would not be any problems from anesthesia. Looking at the MRI, we noticed the tumor looked larger than at the Littleton Hospital. This was very scary. It had grown quite a bit in just a couple of days. Later I would find out that the tumor I had grew fast.

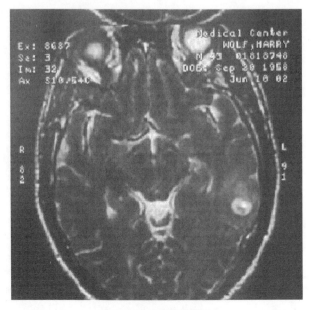

**June 10, 2002 MRI**

I then returned back to the preparation room and they put on what they called Lifesavers®. The surgeon and the computers use the Lifesavers to show the location in my head where the needle biopsy needs to happen. My head had to be shaved to put the Lifesavers on.

It was now 9:00 a.m. and time to get the antibiotics to finish the preparations for surgery. I received Ancef® and Cefazolin® injections. Ancef and Cefazolin are types of antibiotics that were used to protect against infection. The anesthesiologist, surgeon, and nurse had me sign the consent forms. If you have ever had to read these forms, you would find out how scary they really are.

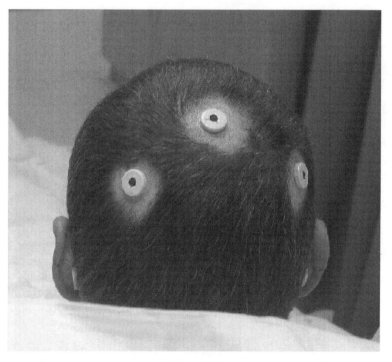

**Lifesavers**

I entered surgery at 10:05 a.m. and was out by 11:45 a.m. The pain was pretty bad and I was given morphine to ease the pain. I was returned to my room at 2:30 p.m. and continued on the Vicodin® pain medication, Cefazolin and 300mg of Dilantin®. I had been taking

Dilantin since day one to prevent future seizures. The Dilantin will become more interesting later. The real key to any man in the hospital was realized at 7:35 p.m. Yes, that is when I made my first pee!!

I had problems with mental capacity and a very bad headache in the hospital. I did not sleep at all and I was very worried about the results of the surgery. The doctor stated that it would take three days to get the final results and thus be able to find out the best way to attack the tumor.

I had an appointment set up for June 12 with my neuro-oncologist, Dr. Arenson. I got out of the hospital on June 11. I took home some pain medicine and had to stay on steroids to help with the swelling. The next step was the June 12 meeting to get the results of the biopsy.

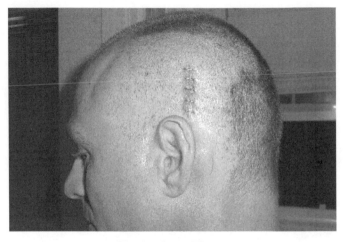

**Staples from Biopsy**

The following sources give a lot of information on brain tumors and could be very helpful as you investigate your symptoms.

Brain Tumors: A Guide
National Brain Tumor Foundation
414 Thirteenth Street, Suite 700 Oakland, CA 94612-2603
www.braintumor.org

*H. Charles Wolf*

A Primer Of Brain Tumors
American Brain Tumor Association
2720 River Road
Des Plaines, IL 60018-4110
e-mail: info@abta.org

# Chapter 2

# *A Little about Charlie*

What drives people? Do we understand what keeps people going? How do people react to death? What do you do if you no longer have a long life, and are now facing death head on?

Who is Charlie Wolf? Why is he writing this book? I started the book because I wanted to share the information I learned and hopefully help others as they battle this disease. I also believe that I was lucky enough to deal with this terrible disease and wanted to help others. Besides, since it is my book, I get to write about myself as well.

Charlie Wolf was born the oldest of five children to Harry Charles Wolf, Senior, and Patricia Ann Wolf on September 20, 1958 in Amherst, Ohio. I grew up like most people did in the 1960's and 1970's with a very strong family relationship. Most holidays and vacation activities involved the family. We drove to my Grandmother's house every Sunday with the rest of the family. Education and hard work were fundamentals. We never had a lot of money, but we were never poor either. As a typical youngster, I wanted to grow up to be an astronaut or the president of the United States.

**Baby Charlie**

As a child there were a few events that had major effects on the way I grew up. One of the key events driving my personality occurred after making a little league team. Most kids my age played baseball. We played all the time in the neighborhood. My friends and I played on the fields near my house every day.

I made the Little League team because I was good enough to be out of the minor leagues. At 8 years old, this was a big deal to be playing up a level. Especially, since I was small in stature. However, the coach decided I was too little to play so I only played the minimum amount of innings. That year was very disappointing and could have put me in the position to quit, but I didn't. I made up my mind at that time that the more I was told I couldn't do it, the more I would prove I could. I think this drove me forward.

The next year, the coach did not have the nerve to tell me before the season had started, that I wasn't going to be playing on his team. So he cut me, and did not tell me in time to work out for another team. As such, I didn't get to try out for the other Little League teams because I thought I was already on a team. I ended up being sent to the Minor League. This turned out to be the best thing that could have happened. I ended up on a good team with a great coach.

My dad worked with me and always believed in me, and I did really well in the minors. That was the start of a very successful baseball career. I had a great time and I was the star of the minor league team. I set a record for home runs, and developed a neat knuckle ball from a neighbor who had actually played in the pros. I had a great time and really developed my confidence.

Ironically, the old Little League team coach wanted me back the next year and was claiming he had waivers. My Dad let him know in no uncertain terms that that would not be the case. I enjoyed playing against my old team every time we faced them. My new team won most of the games against my old team, too. I even pitched a no hitter and won against them. I played baseball throughout high school, but not on the school team.

I could tell several other baseball stories, but they are almost all the same. I always played full out. Some stories about me playing baseball from friends in Chapter 5 are quite interesting.

I played on the 8th grade football team as well. I really enjoyed football, but my size was not the best for football. However, I was tough and never gave up. I played defense and was famous for a real stick on a very large opponent. My size limited me to only an 8th and 9th grade football career.

I also went into wrestling in the 9th grade. That was probably one of the best things I did. I started out the season at 105 pounds and finished the season at 136 pounds. My growth spurt happened in the 9th grade. It was great that I hit my growth spurt here, but it wasn't very good for keeping weight. Making weight was very important for wrestlers; I didn't fit here very well either.

Track ended up being the key sport for me in high school. I became a sprinter my sophomore year. I had the typical sprinter body: short, fast muscles. I lettered for all three years and set a lot of records for my high school. I really enjoyed track because you competed against an opponent as a member of your team. They depended on you and you on them.

I also have a very strong work ethic. I started mowing lawns when I was eight and had some tough work on the weekends. I umpired baseball games as well. That was the way I made my money.

I had a lot of friends in school and was elected class president my freshman year and student council president after that. Although, I knew a lot of people, I did not have what you'd call a best friend or even close friends.

I had a dog when I was little and it died. Her name was Lady. She was my pet from birth to 8 years old. I didn't have much luck with dogs after that. I got a new puppy when we lived on Maple Street. I was walking it across the street when it ran out in front of a car and was killed in front of me. I screamed so loud that the neighbors thought I was hit by the car. The entire block showed up to see what had happened.

**My Dog Lady**

I then had a German Shepard that had to be given away since it bit my sister. I also saw two other puppies run over in front of me and a little dachshund kicked by the neighbor. I think the deaths and how the dogs were killed made things harder for me to develop friends.

I also enjoyed playing golf with my Dad and my brother. We weren't very good and we played on a dog patch course, but we had fun! We would play without a shirt and in tennis shoes. Typical Ohio golf, not the fancy courses that my brother and I play on now.

I worked at Ford Motor Company for two summers while I was in high school. That taught me a lot about work and showed me that I wanted to go to college. I learned various jobs. It was very tough work and very monotonous. I met a lot of great people and learned how to work. The work there finally drove me to be an engineer.

I attended The Ohio State University and majored in Chemical Engineering. I really enjoyed math and chemistry and was pretty good. I started in the Honors Dorm and got straight A's that first year. School was not easy for me. I had to study a great deal to keep up. Again, setting the stage for future work.

I was pretty nerdy my first year in college. The next year I moved into a coed dorm. The guys and girls were on separate floors in the same building. This was a lot more fun. My grades weren't as good, but my social skills greatly improved.

Our dorm decided to enter the intramural games. I ended up winning the Ohio State Intramural 60-meter and 100-meter dashes in 1979 – mainly because Kathy, my future wife, was watching the meets. I also beat some football stars: Ron Springs, who eventually played for the Dallas Cowboys, and Ray Griffin, and Todd Bell. My name was entered into the intramural records book. This was one of the major highlights of my track career. It also showed me that with the right drive you could do anything. I used this as an example of how I could beat the odds with my brain tumor.

**Some Track Medals**

While at Ohio State, I met my wife Kathy. That was probably the single best thing that ever happened to me. She lived on the floor above mine. She was quite a bit different from my quiet pattern, but we hit it off immediately. I was trying to study for an exam and Kathy was making a lot of noise on our floor, as was usual for her. I finally had enough and said, "Shut the f—k up and get the hell off my floor." It was love at first sight and within a month we were inseparable.

In fact, we were so inseparable that we got married September 14, 1979. I was married in my leisure suit with my Afro hairdo. (Now I am completely bald as a result of my chemo treatments!) We spent our honeymoon in the Elyria Holiday Inn since we had to start back to school the following day.

We lived in an apartment in the worst neighborhood in Columbus, Ohio: Indianola and E. 8th Ave. Kathy fed moths in the Entomology Department for some money and my scholarships covered the rest. We couldn't afford to heat the whole apartment even though it only had 3 rooms. We had to put plastic over the windows and room doors to help save money. We even turned our pilot light off at night. We would save our money to collect $10.00 so that we could have a date and play video games. Video games were about the only date we could afford.

Our first daughter, Amber was born on March 14, 1980. We were now a family and Amber was a joy.

Our apartment was a quarter of a house. We were on the top right and our neighbor was next to us. One day he jumped over and said that someone was beating up the guys below him. We called the police, but then did not hear anything. Usually the Columbus police were pretty quick. I finally looked out the front window and heard the sound of a shotgun being cocked. The police SWAT officer waved me back in. I told Kathy to take the baby and stand in the corner. I then looked out the back and saw the entire street was blocked off and the SWAT team was all over.

A little later, the police came in and told us it was a guns-for-drugs deal and that they thought there was going to be a shootout. Everything worked out OK, but we decided that was not a safe place to stay. We moved as soon as possible, to an apartment around the corner.

I did well in school and had a lot of recruitment trips to see which job I would be taking. I chose DuPont at the Savannah River Plant in Aiken, South Carolina. We wanted to move to a warmer place and the job seemed to be the most challenging and unique. I had 16 plant trips and received 15 job offers. I took the offer that would give me the toughest job, which was with DuPont.

My first assignment was with the Savannah River Laboratory to help develop a glass melter for the disposition of high-level radioactive waste. This plant later became the Defense Waste Processing Facility (DWPF). I also worked on the development of the Saltstone Facility, which cemented low-level radioactive waste.

I decided that I wanted to leave the Laboratory job for one that I considered more challenging. I transferred to a position within a group called Separations Technology, responsible for the precipitator in FB-Line. The precipitator was one of the most important steps in the process of making plutonium. I was lucky to be working for a good mentor, Herb.

Herb started to ask me about six times a day how many precipitations did we do and at what rate. Every time I told him what I knew, he always knew more about it. So, I decided the only way I could know more than Herb was to stay out in the facility all day. In fact, I would dress out and stay in the precipitator room. Dressing out means that you put on protective clothing for going into radiation areas. I also wore a respirator and mask as protection against contamination. After a while, Herb really gained confidence in me and I was able to do the job the way I wanted. I learned a lot from Herb. Besides knowing how to run the job, you also needed to understand what the boss needed to know.

The operators in FB-Line were all great guys. I dressed out with the operators everyday. I told them I would teach them why things worked and they could teach me how things worked. When on call, if there was a problem at night, the shift supervisor would have to call me to get approval to take an action outside the approved procedures. I would almost always get a call late at night to help resolve an issue. One shift manager, Alan, gave me a call one night and said we had a spill. I asked, "How much?" He said he didn't know. I told him to go check. He called back and said, "About two liters." I asked, "What color is it?" (The color of plutonium is important because it would tell you what the form and concentration was.) Well, Alan and I went back and forth like that for half the night to resolve the problem. Finally, I told him that if I ever became the Operations Manager, he would call the on-call support only after he had all the necessary information and had a proposed solution. About one month later I became the Operations Manager for FB-Line!

I had been given the choice to become the Operations Manager or the Technical Manager. I chose the more difficult job with more responsibility. Later the positions were combined and I became the Facility Manager. Even as Manager, I still dressed out every day and walked down the facility. That helped me to understand what was going on and take care of worker issues. Before long, we were producing material at record pace, but with the best safety record at the site.

In 1989, the Secretary of Energy stopped operations in all nuclear facilities in the Department of Energy Complex. Therefore, I was in charge of the facility when the United States produced the last plutonium-239 buttons for weapons manufacturing.

In 1990, the HB-Line Facility needed to be restarted to make plutonium-238 to provide fuel for the Cassini space mission to Saturn.

Plutonium-238 is an isotope of plutonium that can serve as a long-lived heat source that can be used to generate electricity for deep-space satellites. I was selected by the company president to be the Facility Manager.

Usually, I requested the toughest jobs that were available. And here we were required to start this facility up while the entire nuclear complex was shut down. We had multiple agencies and groups reviewing every minute detail of the startup. We did succeed to support the Cassini launch. My team and I received several awards from the Department of Energy and NASA.

I spent about 14 years at Savannah River where I worked at a number of other areas including F-Canyon and the Facility Evaluation Board (FEB). The FEB was responsible for overseeing the operations of the facilities for site management. The jobs were a lot of fun and I was lucky enough to have some of the best people working with me. I learned a lot from each and every person I met.

In 1995, my wife and I took another major challenge by going to Rocky Flats in Colorado to remove all the nuclear materials and shut the place down. This was the first time this would happen in the United States. I was responsible for cleaning up the liquid in Building 771. Again I got the best assignment, which was the most difficult. Building 771 was a great facility to work in. The work was very dangerous and difficult, so people looked out for each other.

I was responsible for removing all the liquid radioactive material from the building called "America's Most Dangerous Building" by Peter Jennings. It was given that name by the Plutonium Working Group on Environmental, Safety and Health Vulnerabilities Associated with the U.S. Department of Energy's Plutonium Storage in 1994. That is a lot of words, but it explains the importance of the cleanup.

**Giving Senator Wayne Allard and Staff a Tour of Building 771**

We were very successful in the cleanup of Building 771 and then moved to the 779 building and removed all the gloveboxes and eventually tore it down. Gloveboxes were used in nuclear facilities to protect the workers working with the material. Working at Rocky Flats allowed me to help close the nuclear cycle. I had been in charge of making the nuclear material at Savannah River and now at Rocky Flats we were closing the facility and shutting things down.

I also liked to play around with the stock market in my spare time. I did okay in the market and always wanted to be in the Wall Street Journal. I had been talking to one of their major editors for a while and on March 10, 2000, one of my dreams was answered. I made the front page! It was kind of strange because that was the point the market started to drop and it really hasn't started to improve until now.

**Meeting Archie Griffin, Ohio State's Two-Time-Heisman Winner, in 2000**

Getting back to my work assignments. After the Rocky Flats assignments, I went to the tough jobs Washington Group needed to handle. This led to a six-month job at Fernald in Cincinnati, Ohio and then a second job at Cape Canaveral. Because of my past record, I was given a completely different assignment to work at Cape Canaveral. I was to help get a project back on track. The project was to build a launch pad for Boeing's Evolved Expanded Launch Vehicle (EELV).

During the summer of 2000 our company took over the EELV project in an acquisition from Raytheon. During that December, Lorin, a co-worker, and I went to check it out for the company. We went to Cape Canaveral and when we got back we tried to explain to management how good each other would be for the job (neither one of us wanted the job). As it turned out, we were both assigned to the project. I was assigned Project Manager and Lorin, my deputy. Originally, I was only supposed to be there for three months, so Kathy moved back to Denver.

As Kathy moved into our new house in Denver, it was snowing. I called her from Florida to tell her that we had to evacuate the pad due to another launch. We were at the beach cooking steaks, watching the launch. That didn't go over well since she was dealing with the movers and the snow!

**Fishing in Florida**

As it turned out I spent about 9 months there. The project was very interesting. The launch pad was for a new series of unmanned rockets. The most complex of the rockets is the Delta IV that can lift payloads up to 24,460 pounds. The first EELV vehicle was successfully launched in January 2003 and made me feel proud that I had helped in the success.

Following the Florida job, I was offered the job as Project Manager Functional Lead to help Washington Group on all of its projects. We were making a lot of progress and I thought the work was going to be very helpful. Less than a year into the job, the tumor interfered and soon replaced work with the toughest battle I now face. I kept the job as a major interest, even though I couldn't really work. It was very difficult for me to see my colleagues and friends making things happen for the company when I could not participate.

Since I'm so competitive, I convinced the doctor to let me return last fall, but unfortunately I ended up in the hospital and back out of work. Now I am working hard to recover from this disease. The doctors and my family are working to be sure I am around long enough to enjoy both my family and my job. It finally really came to me that I had to address my tumor and save my life first.

# *Chapter*
# *3*

# *I Saw My Brain!*

On the morning of June 12, 2002 I noticed some memory problems when I woke up. I was at home and was trying to work on my computer. I ended up deleting my AOL (America On-Line) account. AOL helped me get it back on. I also didn't remember a number of other items or passwords. I now realized that the removal of the tumor would not be the only battle. I would also have to deal with brain damage caused by the tumor, the biopsy and future surgeries.

That afternoon we were sitting in Dr. Arenson's waiting room when Dr. Fullagar, my surgeon, walked in. He stated that he didn't have time to talk, but surgery was going to be set up. We knew that was bad news. Then Dr. Arenson's nurse, Mary, called us in. I don't remember much after he said that it was a glioblastoma multiforme, grade 4 out of 4. He informed us that it was the worst kind of brain cancer you can get in the worst location in the brain. Immediate surgery followed by radiation therapy and chemotherapy was the only options. They handed us a book outlining the Colorado Neurological

Institute (CNI) group and the way they handled the treatments. The group had a team approach that we really liked and the team members all seemed very good. I was crying as he announced the verdict and discussed the issues.

The doctor has stated that surgery is the most important part of the treatment and gave me the best chance for survival. My age and health should also be very helpful in fighting the tumor. I will be taking MRI's for the rest of my life every 8 weeks to see how things are going.

I remembered that I had looked up glioblastoma multiforme in several different locations, including the American Brain Tumor Association (ABTA) web site and knew that the statistics showed I only had a 1% chance of living more than 1 to 2 years. All I could think about was that I was going to die and die very soon based on the information I read on glioblastoma statistics.

I decided at this time I was going to fight like crazy, but it was very difficult to not see what looked like reality. As we drove home, I was crying all the way. This was quite a blow in an area that I did not know how to fight. Over a quick 10-day period, I went from perfect health and a strong future to facing death and a tough fight for life ahead of me.

I wrote a note to my family when I got home that night.

> *Family,*
>
> *I am really sorry that I had to inform you that I was dying. You all know me and know I will stick around as long as possible, but unfortunately, not as long as I would like. I have no regrets what so ever and have loved each and every one of you more than you can believe. You all need to hold in there for me and for each other as things move forward. You are all very strong and the best thing for me is for you to continue. I will start writing to each of you for special occasions and am just happy you were all old enough to know me.*

I then wrote some private letters that will not be shared. At this point I thought I had a lot of things I needed to do. I promised my granddaughter, Taylor, we would drive to the beach on her 16th birthday when she can drive. I have two daughters that I need to see their weddings and their kids. I didn't have much hope at this time and thought the statistics would win. That's when I started my theme for this book: "Damn the Statistics, I Have a Life to Live!"

The mental images were also very difficult to face. My Father died on the day of the Oklahoma City Federal Building bombing. I was traveling in the air during that disaster to go to my father's funeral. In 2001, the Word Trade Center was attacked on the day of my Grandmother's funeral. Two deaths in our family had occurred on days of crises that people would not forget. Now, while I was going through the biopsy, the worst fires in Colorado history were happening! Over 100,000 acres had burned in the Hayman Fire and a fire outside Glenwood Springs. I thought my time was coming too.

The next day, after staying up all-night and dealing with my fears and realizing that won't work, I decided to take action into my own hands. Dr. Ravi had mentioned earlier that he did not know Dr. Fullagar, but he knew a neurosurgeon at the University of Colorado. We got an appointment set up for June 20th. I didn't want just one opinion. I wanted to be sure I gave myself the best options available. I also received a call on June 13th, from Kassie, Dr. Fullagar's assistant. She called to tell me she was working with Dr. Fullagar on the MRI and surgery plans.

I began having some vision problems. I didn't know what the cause was, but I became worried. I also got my hair cut by Kathy. She cut my hair pretty short so it wouldn't look too strange. The left side of my head had been shaved due to the biopsy. I also got to take a shower for the first time since the biopsy. It felt great. Kathy took a photo of the staples on my head. I even showed Taylor my staples. We wanted to be sure she wasn't too scared. It turns out that she wasn't scared at all. It is pretty amazing that children love people for who they are and not what they look like.

**With Mike, Sally, and Kathy at Pikes Peak**

Sally and Mike, my sister and her husband, came to visit. I was really glad. It had been so tough since I found out about my tumor and having them visit really cheered me up. Having family and support is really great. It is also nice to discuss your worries and concerns. I am just very anxious waiting for the surgery.

On June 14th, I called Kassie to get the surgery schedule. I called her every day. I was probably extremely aggravating, but it was my life! I understand what the doctors and nurses are trying to do and after working with Kassie later, I now know how hard she was working. But I'm not sure they understand how much stress the patients endure as they wait for their surgery to be scheduled and then more stress when it actually takes place. These were some of the toughest days and nights – waiting to find out the surgery date. Once it is understood things are moving, things are easier to address. (The night after I found out when my surgery was scheduled I slept that I had in a long time. I even thought I dreamed!)

Kathy and I talked to an attorney on the phone. We had to start to get our estate in position in case I didn't make it. It was a tough thought. But I wanted to be sure we were in control of our destiny, not the tumor. All the medications I had been taking as well as the biopsy really made my ability to understand everything that was going on very difficult. I had to read through things multiple times to get a good understanding of what I was reading.

June 15<sup>th</sup> was a very bad day for me. I was hoping that I would get my surgery scheduled for the next couple days, instead I found out it would take weeks to get set up. It really scared me to wait because I knew how fast this tumor grew and that waiting a couple of weeks was very risky. I have been trying to deal with my pending operation, but it was tough to be positive.

My family has really been great support. They had helped me battle through the problems of getting my surgery scheduled. I really appreciated what they did over those days. It is amazing how much family support can help. You could even see how well it was helping my daughters. I continually worried about them and Kathy and how much this was affecting them.

The situation also drives tough thoughts as well. I could only think about that under the current circumstances I will miss a major part of their lives. I feel lucky to have such a wonderful family and to have had the opportunity to enjoy them all for as long as I have. I love Kathy so much and worry how to keep hers and my spirits up. I started a box with letters and things that I wish to say to the family in case the worst happens. On the other hand, I look forward to opening each of them myself and celebrating them. That would be the best way, alive and reading them myself!

I was still not sleeping much. I slept about 2 to 3 hours a night and would walk to the bathroom window and look outside for hours. I think part of it was the heavy medication such as Decadron® (a steroid), and the rest was just thinking about what was happening to me. It is still really weird to know that my life is limited. You feel fine for a while and then realize that things have changed dramatically.

The night of June 17<sup>th</sup>, I really lost it. The fear was just incredible. Everything just kind of ran in at once. I had to keep pushing myself to remain positive. I will beat this and have set my mind to do it. I am not ready to go as I have too many things that I have to see and do.  It is hard to keep pushing, but the alternative is much worse.

It is amazing some of the things you think about.  Charlotte came over one day and helped me by cutting the old man hairs on my eyebrows.  I had a few eyebrow hairs that were very long.  I don't have that problem now.  We also took a walk where I was able to explain how proud I was with her, especially how she handled moving from Ohio and starting school at the University of Colorado.

On June 20$^{th}$, we gathered my MRIs and went to the University of Colorado Neurosciences Center.  We met with the neurosurgeon at 5:30 p.m.  After an evaluation and review of my MRIs, he stated he would not operate.  He thought that my tumor was in a location too dangerous to perform surgery.  He was concerned that I would be unable to speak or that I would suffer from other problems that may diminish my quality of life.  He offered us a chance to enter their research program.  But without surgery, I did not have a very good chance for a long life.  That was a real blow to me.  It was a good thing that Dr. Fullagar had already stated he would operate or I don't know what I would have done.

Stephanie really helped me that night.  I was feeling really low and crying at about one in the morning.  She came down and sat with me on the couch and we talked about my illness for a couple of hours.  This was a very important time for me, and Stephanie was great.

On June 21, 2002, trying to keep things moving, I met with Dr. Marsh Davis, the radiation oncologist.  He explained the CNI program very well and again gave me more confidence that I had the right team.

Three days later I met with Dr. Fullagar.  I was informed that surgery was set for July 1$^{st}$.  I was really relieved a date had been set.  He then led me through the process of how they would map my brain functions.  First I would receive the general anesthetic and then the skullcap would be removed.  Next I would be woken up for the awake craniotomy and once that was completed, I would be put back to sleep for the tumor removal.  (I have more details later.)  It was kind of strange to be happy to get your head cut open, especially while you were awake.  But I finally had my operation set.  The surgery was supposed to be the most important part of my survival, so I was glad it was finally scheduled.

Amber had her turn to start early support on June 24th. We went to the lake near our old house to go fishing. We all went, Amber, Alan (Amber's husband), Taylor, Charlotte, Stephanie, Kathy, and me. There were no fish, but it was the family time that was great. I needed a break and I needed normal activities. Fishing at the lake had always been a fun activity for us and we had a blast. Doing normal activities is key and that proved to be important later on. Do them!

The next day I went boating on Chatfield Reservoir for the first time with one of my friends, John L. It was fun. Kathy and I had a good time and I really enjoyed the day. This is another example of trying to enjoy normal activities. I needed normal activities to keep sane.

Later that afternoon, I was pretty depressed again. The steroids and other medication along with other things were keeping me anxious again. I wanted to be able to leave something for the kids. My sister Sally prepared some books for me to record information on the kids' lives and I wanted to be sure that each kid got one. Sally and her husband Mike made these books for me since I got upset when I couldn't find anything in the stores to help me do this. Remember, I was on high Decadron doses and sleeping about 2 hours a night, so I got agitated very easily.

On June 26th, we had a party at my house with Taylor. In fact, she wrote in my book "Taylor and Papa Charlie had a party." We went to the grocery store and picked up some ice cream and set our pillows up in the family room to watch TV. We watched a really bad movie called *Tremors 3*. Taylor really loved it because the monsters were called "butt blasters." We also had a good time blowing bubbles with some bubble guns that we picked up at Wal-Mart. The bubble guns blew bubbles hundreds at a time. Charlotte stopped by and the three of us really had fun with the bubbles. As my operation neared, it was great to have fun and forget about it for a while.

**With My Daughters, Stephanie and Charlotte, before Surgery Day**

On June 28th, I met with Dr. Jay Schneiders. Dr. Schneiders was a health psychologist and neuropsychologist. He gave me even more details on the operation and did various tests for the awake craniotomy. He asked me the questions they would ask during the awake craniotomy and told me how it would work. He also asked me a number of questions to be sure he understood the sound of my voice and how I spoke.

Dr. Schneiders led us through what occurred in my brain. The tumor resulted in dysnomic parial gerstman syndrome, finger agnosia neologism, significant acalculia, left-right confusion, left temporal parietal lesion. After all that, I was told I didn't have hemipiparesis. I was sure glad that at least I didn't have something. I felt comfortable with him and again, he was another member of the CNI team. I have dedicated an entire chapter to the issues associated with the brain problems after surgery.

As surgery time came closer, I was even more nervous and I wanted to get the surgery over with. I didn't know what would happen during surgery or how to prepare for it. I also didn't know what to expect afterwards. Kathy and Stephanie took me out to dinner at Outback and then we rented the movie, *A Beautiful Mind*. I really enjoyed the movie and had tears in my eyes as I watched it.

The main character in that movie had problems similar to the minor ones I had with my brain. I didn't realize that I still had a long way to go.

My daughter, Amber, had contacted a lot of my friends by e-mail and created a *Recovery Book* for me. As I read through the book, I laughed and cried. I talk more about it in the chapter, "Family and Friends, They Keep you Going."

I didn't sleep at all the night before surgery because I was scared. They were operating on my brain and removing a large part of my brain and the surgery was to occur in my speech center. I was really worried about dying or being paralyzed or not being able to speak. I was worried about me, but even more concerned about my family and what would happen to them if my surgery didn't go well. I could deal with whatever happened, but I didn't know how my family would deal with this.

Waiting for this surgery had me thinking about the potential for death and making sure that people were aware. I wrote letters to each of my kids and my wife to read if I did not make it. I also sent e-mails to a few close friends as well. This is the night I also started my journal.

Here is the note I sent to my friends by e-mail. I wrote it with tears running down my eyes, but wanted to be sure if I didn't make it, I had a chance to say something before it was too late.

> *Friends,*
>
> *Today I enter into a surgery where the doctors say there is a potential that my cognitive functions, speech or motion may be impacted. So obviously, I have to say something before then. Some of you are aware my father died within 1 month of being diagnosed with a brain tumor in 1995 and never was able to speak after his initial stroke. They also tell me that statistically only 1% of people with glioblastoma multiforme survive greater than 1-2 years. They say they have to tell me this to prevent false hope. It's a good thing I am approaching this like a project where failure is unacceptable and if you plan it out properly and execute*

that plan properly, your rate of success rises dramatically. So far I have chosen this team like all my teams in the past, they are smarter than me, more talented than me, and more aggressive than me, but I have set the vision and I will enforce the standards of performance.

I always thought I would be thinking of my mortality at 100 or I would go quick and not worry about it. Having almost a month now knowing I had a tumor and 2 weeks knowing I had one that without surgery would kill me within 3-6 months was a very sobering event and since I couldn't drink due to all the anti-seizure medication and other massive amounts of steroids and drugs it really was sobering.

I want to thank you for your e-mails, letters, cards, gifts, phone calls, and contributions to the Recovery Book my daughter Amber pulled together. This has kept me focused and ready to beat this. I really enjoyed reading a lot of stories and letters from past assignments and life events. It has helped me think about things. The famous "they" always say that nobody ever wishes they worked more. Well, if I had everything to do over knowing exactly what I know now. I would still be in my office on June 3, 2002 at 0930 starting this nightmare all over again.

The reason is work was never work for me. I always had a great time because of all the fantastic people I got to work with. They were part of my family and in many cases my family was indistinguishable from them. Some of them can tell you more about me and my kids than I can and I can tell you more about their golf games, which minor league ball players they know, which colleges their daughters attend, how their back surgery went or what their master's degree topic was. I know in detail the statistics of the stellar SSOC indoor soccer season where we were outscored by an average of 22-1 per game, but never gave up and there are more than enough stories on my ability to use my head while playing softball. We kept bands from playing in Florida because it interfered with the Stanley Cup Playoffs last year at the Cape and introduced Cleveland to the AVS this year while preparing project management training.

I was lucky enough to work on some really cool assignments with some great folks. We worked with SRTC on Saltstone with people who first taught me how to be an engineer. I worked with some of the greatest minds of the century and workers as we produced the last weapons grade Pu-239 to support our nations defense. We also started up the Pu-238 facility to make material for Cassini when the entire weapons complex was being shutdown. At Rocky we did things that nobody thought was possible and changed the entire way people thought and had fun for the first few years. And recently, the operations center concept, functional leads, and corporate reorganization have forged a great company out of bankruptcy. In each and every one of these assignments, besides working with some of the best people I ever knew, I was lucky enough to work for the greatest set of managers and bosses that anyone could ask for starting at Savannah River and throughout my career, I was lucky enough to work for bosses that really cared for their work force. Lastly, besides the awake craniotomy I am going to try and persuade the doctors to actually let me see my brain. I think that would be so cool and would give me stories for years!

Since I was 7 years old if anyone told me something could not be done, I tried 20 times harder to prove him or her wrong. I do not like to lose and very rarely did. Whether it was running full speed into an outfield fence to catch a home run that was already 40 feet over or setting the 60 meter dash intramural record at Ohio State in the winter of 78 and the 100 meter intramural record in the spring of 79 to impress a young lady (Kathy). I won the 100-meter after Ron Springs later of Dallas Cowboy fame and Ray Griffin that year stated that they didn't think I even belonged on the track.  I also had a story on me on the front page of the *Wall Street Journal* in March of 2000 and wrestled a 60 lb hammerhead shark in from shore so he wouldn't break my test line.  I am rambling probably as much to get myself pumped up for tomorrow, but I have beaten the odds before and I fully intend on beating them again and the main reason is because of the wonderful network of family and friends that I have.  I am not ready to give up my relationships with any of these people any time soon.

I am not sure what the best way is (a phone call, an e-mail), but please be sure my family is taken care of on Monday and early in the week.  We arrive at Swedish Hospital Monday at 7:00 and start procedures by 7:30 and surgery is expected to last potentially as long as 6:00 at night.  I am not sure what form of Frankenstein I will look like or sound like after surgery and they may need a few familiar voices to talk to.  If nothing else maybe some of the old SSOC guys could cheer her up with the Hungry Dog speech.  I am sure it is posted on each and every one of your bulletin boards.

Charlie

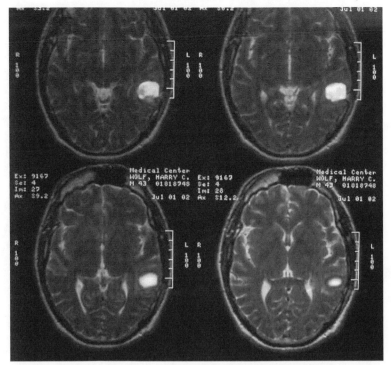

**View of Tumor, July 1, 2002, before Surgery**

We checked into Swedish Medical Center for surgery at 7:00 a.m. on July 1, 2002. At 8:00 a.m. the MRI was started and I was back to the preparation room by 8:50 a.m. I was starting to get used to this practice. Antibiotics, surgery socks, and then Dr. Schneiders stopped by at 9:10 a.m. to check on my reading comprehension, to go over some words, and to again review his part of the operation. At 10:00 a.m., I received some Versed® for relaxation and was taken into the operating room. My wife would be taking the notes from here.

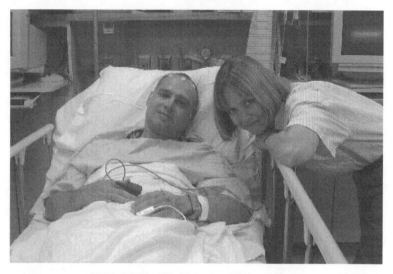

**With Kathy Waiting for Surgery**

At 1:00 p.m., Debbie, my nurse, called Kathy to let her know they were just beginning the awake craniotomy. The process requires a lot of time for set up and removal of the brain cap. At 2:00 p.m., Dr. Schneiders and Dr. Phillips stopped by and said that I had some epileptic episodes in the brain when they first started the open craniotomy. They said that no motor areas were affected and that I told them to say that things were fine. He even discussed with Kathy the story I told him about throwing her out of my dormitory floor at Ohio State. I am sure this version was a little tamer.

Debbie called again at 2:45 p.m. stating that I was okay, but that things were going pretty slow. Pam, the social worker of the CNI team, stopped by at 3:45 p.m. to say they were wheeling me out of surgery and I looked good. At 4:15 p.m., another nurse, Rene, came out of the recovery room. She said my speech was a little garbled, but I knew where I was (Swedish) and could count to 5. She also stated that it looked like only good brain tissue was left behind.

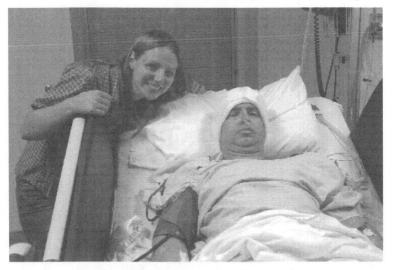

**With My Daughter Amber after Surgery**

At 5:00 p.m., I was moved to the Intensive Care Unit (ICU) and Becky became my nurse. Dr. Fullagar stopped in at 5:30 p.m. to give Kathy a status and said things went well and they would give me an MRI tomorrow to verify things. Kathy was told to expect garbled speech, so she should talk to me slowly. I understood right from left and things should improve with speech therapy.

Kathy was allowed to see me at 5:45 p.m. She said I looked good; I could answer questions with one-word answers with no problem, but my speech was garbled with sentences. We were told I would be in a regular room the next day.

The next day, I woke up in the ICU. My speech was still garbled. I needed Zofran® for nausea, Percoset® for pain, Pepsid®, and antibiotics. Dr. Schneiders stopped by at 8:30 a.m. and told Kathy that the speech would improve after the swelling calmed down. She told him how I was better last night. Now, I could not speak. The swelling had gotten worse and was probably causing more speech problems. Then the orderly arrived to take me down for the MRI at 8:35 a.m.

Dr. Fullagar arrived at 10:15 a.m. He thought the speech problems might be a result of some edema. He took out the catheter and told me to try and get up and eat. Edema is just a fancy word for swelling. Things were tough that morning, I could not speak, I

37

couldn't read, and I was in massive pain. This is not what I had expected. I was given Zofran, Decadron and morphine instead of Percoset, since I wasn't eating and had an empty stomach. This was the toughest situation I had gone through in my life. I didn't know if I would ever speak, read, or if I would have additional problems.

Dr. Arenson arrived at 1:00 p.m. and told us he would track down the MRI to see what was up. He was back in 15 minutes and said that the gross tumor had been removed and **we were now headed for the cure!** The pain was still quite intense and I was still on morphine. Vicki from rehab showed up. I could not look at the ceiling when asked, I couldn't read "mama", and I couldn't identify a picture of a chair. This was not a good time for me. I was not able to understand or perform very basic activities. I was trying to keep positive, but with the information to date, I was really fighting depression. The worst part was that I had all my knowledge, but couldn't communicate or understand what was being communicated to me.

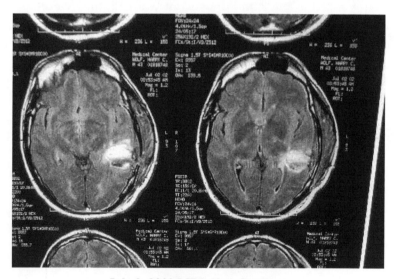

**July 2, 2002 MRI, Note Swelling**

I hit the lowest point at 10:00 p.m. that night. I threw up due to too much morphine. I had not eaten since before surgery, I could not talk except for gibberish, and I could not read! I was very depressed because this was not the outcome I expected.

It got even worse the next day. I was not interacting with Kathy and when the nurse asked me if I knew where I was, I just nodded yes. She then asked if I was in my house and I nodded yes again. I was so depressed and was not sure I would speak or read again. This would be a very tough time for any patient and I needed the hope that things would improve.

July 3rd, at 8:45 a.m., I tried to eat some green gelatin. I wanted to do it myself, despite that I had great difficulty trying to hold the spoon. When I had to go pee, there was no modesty at this point. I just flung off the covers, no matter who was there. It was a surprise the kids didn't expect or enjoy! I still could not communicate and I was very frustrated. I remember my father trying to communicate with his tumor and I now understand how bad it really was. The speech therapist was bringing pictures to try and help. They thought I might be able to communicate through photos.

Later that day, Dr. Fullagar released me from the ICU. He said he was a little concerned, but the swelling probably hadn't peaked yet. I headed to the 9th Floor. I would spend a lot of time on this floor over the next few months. Dr. Schneiders stopped by again at 5:30 p.m. and advised us that singing may help me communicate. Singing gets the right side of the brain working; sometimes you can sing when you can't talk. This was not a trick I used. I was no singer and by this point, I was pretty upset and frustrated by my progress.

The frustration continued that night. I had to pee really quickly. I threw open the covers as usual and grabbed my bedpan. I spilled a little on the bed and was very upset because I could not explain that I needed new sheets. Kathy eventually figured it out. This was a bad situation. I could not even let people know that they had to change my sheets.

By 9:00 p.m. that night, I seemed to understand more. I was still unable to communicate perfectly, but I was trying. I was determined to improve. I could not stand the current situation. The next time I got medicine, I tried to take it orally, but spilled the water all over the bed. I tried to say "God Damn It!" It didn't come out right, but my family could understand it!

July 4th came around. It was three days after surgery and I could still not talk and was very frustrated. I had not eaten yet and had no desire to up to this point. My motor skills were getting better and I could pee in the bottle just fine. There was still the lack of modesty issue; I just flipped open the covers and went! I wondered later if there was a correlation to my ability to speak and my modesty.

For lunch I finally had something to eat. I had some tomato soup, crackers, strawberry ice cream, and carrots. This was excellent! A true meal!

At 3:20 p.m., I woke up, screaming, "It hurts!" That was the first coherent thing I had said and my speech finally started coming back. I then asked, "What time was it?"

One of the saddest things to happen was the inability to remember my kid's names. I called Amber, my oldest daughter, "Sally," who is my sister. My Mom called and she asked about the kids. I said the girl who's a smart ass is here, referring to my youngest, Stephanie. I also said to Amber, "I remember your little girl," meaning Taylor, my granddaughter. I also stated, "I remember the craniotomy." I continued discussing my surgery and said "they let me see my brain and it scared me to death!" I was now talking pretty well and improving every minute.

I went to go pee again at 7:25 p.m. This time I had a lot of modesty. It must be associated with the level of recovery. I also wanted to see my head. I had not seen what had been done yet. The nurse set me up with a mirror. Stephanie said I made funny faces.

That night I asked the nurse if you could see the Fourth of July fireworks from the room. She said that I could not see them from here. I had tears running down my face as I was looking forward to seeing fireworks. I just wanted to see things that were normal again. The fireworks would have been a great help.

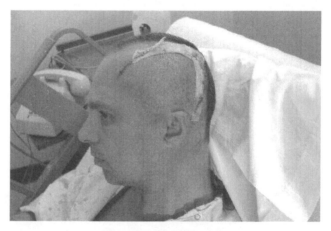

**Stitches from Craniotomy**

At 8:00 a.m. on July 5<sup>th</sup> Dr. Arenson stopped by. I was doing much better and he gave me an anticoagulant shot to prevent blood clots. The therapist checked my vision and said I was just a little slow. She gave me coordination exercises for my right arm and hand.

On July 6, 2002, a speech therapist gave me some exercises to help. The problem was that I could not read at all. That was very scary. Later, we walked down to look at the MRI and could see how much swelling was still present.

I was let out of the hospital about 4:00 p.m. that afternoon. I could not read at this time, but I was glad to get out of the hospital.

# Chapter
4

# *The Goal is Now the Cure!*

Dr. Arenson had stated on July $2^{nd}$, that the gross tumor had been removed! "The goal is now the cure!" I remembered that comment as we entered Dr. Marsh Davis' office to begin the simulation for radiation.

During this session my radiation mask was made for me to wear when I received treatment. I was called back and laid down on the table as they prepared to form the mask to my face. They had put the hot material over my face very tightly. It put me into shock because I was claustrophobic and I was being tied down. They warned me not to move or the mask would have to be redone. They took x-rays, a CAT scan and other measurement with my mask. I was relieved when they finally took off the mask, but I knew I would have to return for the final simulation before the radiation treatments began.

On July $15^{th}$, I went back to Dr. Fullagar's office to have the stitches from the surgery taken out. There were over 57 stitches to be removed and while we were in the office they stated that a few might have to be left in and removed later. They pulled the stitches out and I was thrilled! I could now wash my hair.

The next morning, I noticed some bleeding from where the surgery stitches were removed. By about noon, there was a lot of leaking from that area, so we called Dr. Fullagar's office. They said to come right in. Dr. Fullagar noticed that there was fluid collecting on that side of my head. He squeezed that area of my head to push more of the liquid out.

My head just "gushed like a water gun," as described by my daughter Charlotte. I don't understand how she could watch. He then sewed it back up with two stitches. Since I was in such pain, he could do it without anesthetic. They put on a pressure bandage and it looked like things were ready to go.

**With Pressure Bandage and My Mom, July 16, 2002**

Our instructions were to keep the bandage on until my appointment on July 25th. He would remove the new stitches then. I had radiation practice scheduled for the end of the week and was given the okay to still use my mask then.

On July 18th, my head was still hurting. The previous day and I had woken up at 5:00 a.m. with a massive headache. I took a Vicodin, even though I usually tried not to take pain medication at all.

I took off the pressure bandage because I was in intense pain and my head had swelled immensely. My pain was so intense and no pain medicine helped. My head had swelled bigger than it was after my surgery.

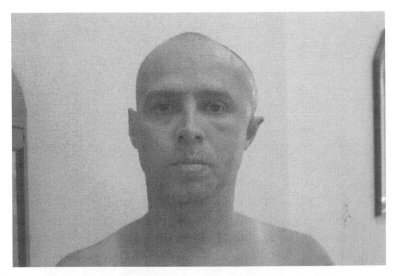

**Swollen Head, July 18, 2002**

We called the doctor's office and told them the pain level I had. I stated the pain was at a level of 32 on a scale of 1 to 10. I could not sit down or do anything. I just paced in the house until we could get into the doctor's office. My mom tried to help, but I told her there was nothing she could do.

We got a hold of Dr. Fullagar's backup, as the other doctors were at the Brain Tumor Day with the Colorado Rockies baseball team. He drained fluid from my head again and thought it looked infected and should be cleaned out. He instructed us to return to the hospital to have the bone plate removed and rinsed.

By 4:00 p.m., we were admitted to the hospital and my labs were taken by 5:00 p.m. Dr. Bartczak, an infectious disease specialist, looked at my head and thought it was a staph infection. She also noticed that my kidney function was a little off, so we needed to watch the dose of drugs. This was a very good observation that helped things out later. I was started on antibiotics that were to be given for a long time. She suggested I might want a "PICC" line in because it can last for months and I would use it. A "PICC" line is short for Peripherally Inserted Central Catheter. It is a long thin catheter inserted in a large vein near the elbow in the arm. It is then pushed into the vein until the tip sits in the large blood vessel that leads to the heart. A "PICC" line would allow me to give blood and get my medications without having to have an IV.

By Friday, July 19th, I had a fever of 102°F, which went down to 98.3°F during the day. Fluoroscopy – live x-ray guidance – was used to put the PICC line in the major vein in my upper arm. The whole CNI team arrived that morning and checked on how things were going. They discussed everything and decided to let the antibiotics work on my infection, trying to avoid another surgery. The doctor then pushed out more fluid from my head and said if it came back, something else would need to be done.

That afternoon about 5:45 p.m., Dr. Schneiders arrived to help me get prepared for my radiation testing. He explained how they had only one shot at the tumor. There were vital areas in a horseshoe shape around the tumor. He told me to call him in the morning and he would help me with relaxation techniques for my radiation treatments, if I got released from the hospital.

The next day, the infectious disease doctor confirmed the staph infection. We thought I was headed out this day. But by 3:30 p.m., I had a severe headache and a fever of 101.7°F.

This was one of the days that were very difficult on the family. My mother, Kathy, and I were in an argument because I was stating that I was going to have to have surgery again. My head was swollen and leaking spinal fluid, I knew I was going to need surgery. My mom and Kathy were really worried that my other therapies would be delayed by the surgery. They thought that I was not looking for a solution, and that I wanted to accept the worst. At this time all was not fine, and my mom got Pam, our patient consultant, to come to talk to us because I was having trouble dealing with it. After talking to Pam, she understood where I was coming from; it was my mother and Kathy who didn't want to think that I needed surgery, which would delay my other therapies.

It didn't take long to see what would really happen. I got a severe headache from the fluid building back up in my head and my temperature rose. The nurse called the infectious disease doctor who ordered more labs and added oxacillin. Oxacillin is a type of antibiotic.

The nurse then called Dr. Fullagar who scheduled surgery for the next morning. The interesting fact was that it was 9:00 p.m. SATURDAY and Dr. Fullagar set surgery for SUNDAY morning at 9:00 a.m. Dr. Fullagar scored additional points with me by acting quickly.

On Sunday, July 21$^{st}$, I woke with a 101.3°F fever and my head was leaking. Dr. Bartczak stopped by – it was staph aureous and the treatment would be changed to a more specific antibiotic. Staph aureous is a common type of staph infection. I was hoping that this would not stop the operation.

I was rolled down for surgery at 9:00 a.m. The anesthesiologist and Dr. Fullagar explained how they would try to take the bone flap out, rinse out my head, and put a drain in. If the bone were mushy (infected), then they would have to leave the bone flap out. At 11:10 p.m., Dr. Fullagar came out and told Kathy that they took the bone flap out, cleaned it up, and put it back in. He said the bone looked good and he didn't want to leave a big hole that they would have to be covered by a plate in 6 months. They put a drain in and sent me to the ICU. The drain was put in to drain fluid from my head.

The next day, I was still in ICU and on oxacillin, and they told me I had to stay in ICU until the doctor came. At 6:00 p.m. I was released to go back to the ninth floor and told I would be on antibiotics for 6 weeks. At midnight I was taken to a room on the 9$^{th}$ floor.

Dr. Bartczak came in about 8:15 a.m. the next day to check on me and Dr. Arenson stopped by around 9:00 a.m. He stated he would order an MRI to see the status of the tumor since things have been delayed a long time due to the infection. He was going to work with the other team members to see when radiation would begin.

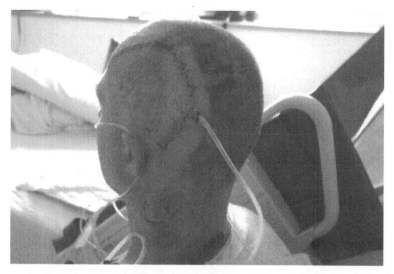

**Charlie the *Borg* with Drain Tube**

It was now July 23rd and Dr. Bartczak found there were problems with my kidneys – my function number was 4.6 – which meant that I was on the brink of kidney failure. A normal reading is 1.0 and I had previously been running 1.2 to 1.4. I really didn't know what the numbers meant, but I knew I was in trouble.

The last thing I needed was to get sicker and delay treatment again. It was beginning to look like nothing was going right. They thought my kidney function number might be incorrect since it was so abnormal. It was a good thing that Dr. Bartczak had continued to follow-up on the problem. If she hadn't, I would have been in real trouble.

At 11:15 a.m., the blood results confirmed that my kidneys were at 4.6 and an ultrasound was ordered to check my kidneys for damage. Dr. Garrett, a kidney specialist, was called in by 12:15 p.m. Although Dr. Garrett would not be your first choice if you saw him on the street, he was excellent and I give him credit for saving my kidneys. The ultrasound was pushed off to the next day and I was not allowed to eat until after midnight.

Dr. Garrett showed up in the morning and set up a recovery plan. My kidneys were now stable, but number was still high. He took me off Zonegran®, which may have caused some of the problems, along with the strong antibiotics, or it may have even been the infection. Zonegran was one of my original seizure medicines. The treatment plan proposed by Dr. Garrett would handle any of these problems.

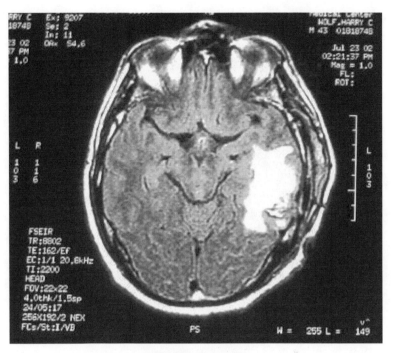

**MRI July 23, 2002**

On July 24th, at 4:30 p.m., Dr. Arenson arrived to discuss the MRI. He told me that the MRI was okay. I knew how much time had passed since the surgery and how fast this tumor grew and I was really worried. I was afraid the tumor would return before I started chemo.

At 6:30, I had an IV started with potassium chloride and multivitamins to flush my system. I had to collect my urine so it could be strained and sent to pathology. This routine lasted until I left the hospital. You can wonder how much the nurses loved to strain my urine all that time. One of the best moments was when I got out of the hospital and could pee in a toilet. At this time I was down to 145 lbs from my original weight of 155 lbs. I started my new seizure medicine, Neurontin®.

When Thursday the 25th rolled around, the drain was taken out of my head. I had looked like a "Borg" from the *Star Trek* program with a tube sticking out of my head. It was amazing how big the drain apparatus and its associated equipment was. "Don't get my head wet for a couple of days" was the major suggestion.

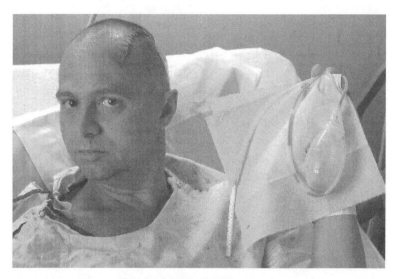

**Drain Apparatus Removed**

I was then taken down to get an ultrasound and a Doppler ultrasound to check my kidneys. Everything seemed to look pretty good. The ultrasounds looked similar to the ones you get for a baby. Luckily, my baby came out okay. This would be pretty cool stuff, if it weren't all happening to me.

I still had a 101°F temperature and was not allowed out of the hospital, another set back. Dr. Bartczak said my kidney function number was down to 3.5 – getting better still, but thought that there was still some vancomycin, the strong antibiotic, in my system. But it should not be in my system too long. I would be on antibiotics for 4 to 6 weeks, including time from surgery. They put me on oxacillin. Oxacillin is much easier on the kidneys and would keep me from getting into more problems. We met with the inpatient social worker to set up home delivery on the antibiotics and home care.

The hospital set up the home care nurse to make sure the PICC line and antibiotics could be handled at home. The nurse would teach us how to handle the antibiotics and teach Kathy how to handle everything associated with the PICC line. This option allowed for short-term additions of medicine or drugs at the hospital or at home, using a portable pump.

I started to do much better with my homework words for speech therapy. Kim from speech therapy was helping with reading exercises. Reading was still very difficult and I still couldn't really read.

The next day was Friday, July 26th, and that meant the whole CNI team would show up for rounds. Everyone was ready to release me on Saturday, if my fever stayed down. Dr. Garrett said if my kidney function readings dropped to 1.0–1.5 by Saturday, he would let me out. Case management arrived and we were all set for home care.

**With Stephanie in the Hospital, July 27, 2002**

Saturday, the 27th, Dr. Garrett decided that I could not get out of the hospital; my kidneys weren't in good enough shape. I had been in the hospital for many days and was ready to get out. I had been pumped to go home. When he said I had to stay until Monday, I cried because I could not go home. It was better for me to stay, but I was really ready to get out.

My temperature had been staying below the fever level for a couple of days as we entered Sunday the 28th. Dr. Garrett showed up again on Sunday. The kidney reading was now at 2.0 and he said I needed to get to 1.6–1.8 to be able to get out. He said if things went well, I could be home by dinnertime on Monday. That was my new goal. The longer I went through this, the more goals became very important. Dr. Garrett explained what I would need to do to get out and I was ready to do it.

Monday arrived and I was ready to be out of the hospital. The nurses checked my creatine (what they measured for kidney function) and it was 1.8. "I was getting out of here," I thought. I had to do a DDAVP test that took 3 hours, before I could escape. DDAVP (1-deamino-8-D-arginine vaso-pressin) is a synthetic analogue of an anti-diuretic hormone. The key for me was that I would get out of the hospital if I passed this test. I also found out that DDAVP is used to help kids from wetting the bed. It just goes to show how medications can have multiple uses. The nurses got me started on the test before the doctor arrived so that I could exit as soon as possible. They knew how badly I wanted to go home.

Dr. Garrett had me drink four Gatorades everyday and take salt tablets. I needed to take a hormone pill (DDAVP) once a day for the next five days at night. At 3:00 p.m. the lab results came back and were good. Dr. Fullagar released me. Appointments were set up with Dr. Fullagar and Dr. Bartczak for the following week. The discharge papers were worked on and I was out by 4:00.

At 7:30 that evening, the home service nurse, Brenda, delivered my PICC line equipment and showed us how to operate it. A pump gave me oxacillin four times a day to ensure that I got the proper amount of medicine. Kathy needed to change the oxacillin supply at night and flush the tubes with heparin, an anticoagulant.

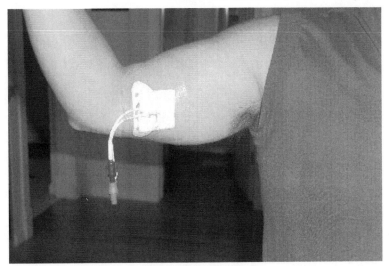

**PICC Line**

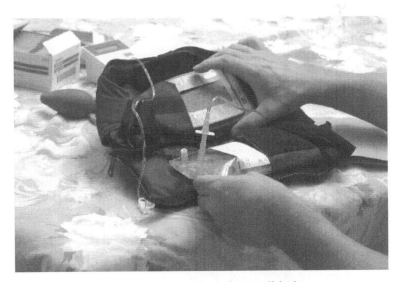

**Pump and Fanny Pack for Antibiotics**

I do not even know how to describe my life over these past two months. I have outlined some of the things that happened, but it has been so horrible, and very hard to describe. I cannot describe the pain and agony that I went through and the agony of what was happening in my life. I was most concerned about how to handle this. My thoughts were that I didn't want to die; I love my family and I didn't want to go. I was starting to realize how difficult my new life would be. I began to realize that it truly is a new life because things can never be the same again.

On August 5$^{th}$, Dr. Fullager removed the first half of my staples from my surgery and gave me approval to have radiation and chemotherapy. On August 6$^{th}$, my first radiation therapy started!!!

Finally after brain surgery, a major infection that I was still fighting, a second surgery to remove infection off the brain flap, a near kidney failure, and 6 weeks of antibiotics, I was finally ready to start working on the CURE!!

# *Chapter*
# 5

# *Family and Friends, They Keep You Going*

My daughter, Amber, made me a Recovery Book. The evening before surgery, she gave it to me. I was a little apprehensive to read it at first, because of the way I might feel. I thought it would be sad seeing how people felt sorry for me. Instead, it was great! I got the biggest laugh and really enjoyed the comments and stories from my friends and family.

Amber had sent e-mails out to people I knew and asked for "Charlie Stories." She was interested to see if anyone had Charlie Stories out there and thought it would help me to read those stories and think of the happier times while going through the rough times in the hospital.

She also thought that the Recovery Book would be a good thing for her mom, sisters, as well as myself, to read through and remember the pre-tumor days. The Recovery Book also allowed my co-workers, family, and friends to send something personal to me.

They could send something to me and feel like they were positively contributing without having to worry about trying to call me or sending the generic sympathy/get-well card.

She got a few e-mail addresses from her mom and began contacting people from there. She sent a letter telling whoever read that e-mail that she was putting a book together for me and for them to send her any get-well notes or funny "Charlie Stories." The e-mail first went to my current secretary, my old secretary, and a few of my friends that the family knew. At the end of the e-mail letter, she added "please pass this on to anyone and everyone who knew my dad." Next thing she knew she began receiving ten to twenty emails a day with stories, get well wishes, and people wanting information on how I was doing.

The Recovery Book was great and really helped me a lot. This is a great idea for people undergoing any type of serious surgery. The first letter was from Amber to me:


*Dad,*

*I hope this cheers you up in bad times and makes you even happier in the good times.*

*You have a tremendous support system with all your friends, coworkers, and family. And we all love you very much and will help you through the bad times. You taught me not to be a quitter and I expect the same from you. No slack!*

*Love,*
*Amber*

**Amber and I at a Much Happier Time**

I wanted to share some of the letters in my recovery book to give people an idea of how well these emails and letters helped me. Most people are used to the short illnesses and hospitalization where you visit or call someone once or twice. But with a brain tumor, the illness lasts the rest of your life. By having these stories with me constantly, it really helps.

> The SSOC co-ed softball team was never competitive but we had fun. I remember when Charlie was in left field and I was shortstop. A pop fly foul ball was hit down the left first line and Charlie, the third baseman, and I converged. Charlie began to dramatically wave us off while yelling, "I've got it". We backed off and witnessed Charlie doing his third dramatic wave (with both arms), just when his arms were completely outstretched to his side, the ball arrived, nailing him directly in the middle of the forehead and knocking him to the ground in a heap. We were lucky it was foul since it is nearly impossible to throw a ball when you are cracking up. When we arrived in the dug out, still wiping tears

from our eyes, we got a second round of gaiety when the bruise appeared, round with the stitches clearly indented on his forehead.

Another time I was playing left-center and Charlie was right-center. The batter smashed a line drive straightaway center. We both turned to run. I saw that it was clearly a homer (by 40 feet), but Charlie, blessed with blinding speed, was going to run it down. When the ball cleared his head he put his head down and turned on the jets. When he was about ten feet from the fence I realized he wasn't going to stop and yelled, "Charlie!" He looked up just in time to hit the chain link fence at full speed! He slingshotted backwards (past me) and landed on his back about 20 feet from the fence. I got there, seeing that he was all right and busted a gut. I was incapable of moving, I was laughing so hard. When the infield arrived to assess his condition they found me choking and him okay but grid marked by the fence. I was labeled as insensitive to his potential injuries, which he promoted so that people wouldn't recognize what he had just done. As usual, Charlie made a mistake while going full tilt and I took the heat. It was worth it to witness the human slingshot!

—Scott S.


*As you know, Grandpa Wolf was big into officiating sports, basketball, baseball, softball, football, etc. As a result of that he encouraged us kids to do the same. One, it was a good experience and two, a chance to make a little extra money. The fact that we only lived 3 blocks from the baseball fields made it convenient as well. And since all five of us played summer baseball or softball the entire family spent a lot of time up at the fields. Anyhow, I was playing a game one-day and Charlie was home plate umpire for another game a couple of diamonds over. My Dad would ride his bike back and forth taking turns watching me and then watching Charlie umpire. I as usual was having a great game; I was 3 for 3 going into the late innings. Dad was cheering me on and said he would be back to see if I could go 4 for 4 or better. I went to the plate, looked around, but Dad was not to be found. I ended up going 4 for 5 but was puzzled as to why Dad did not come back to watch me.*

*The game ended and I went over to Charlie's field and they were just finishing up. Dad wasn't there either. So I asked Charlie where Dad was? He said, "I don't know! He was giving me a hard time on some of my calls so I threw him of the ball park!" I am sure it seemed like a good idea to Charlie at the time, but I was glad I wasn't him on the way home!!*

*—Uncle Rick*

My Good Story on Charlie is when he bid on the Sammy Sosa baseball jersey at a charity function in Denver. It was of course the feature item, and the bid started in the hundreds of dollars. When it go to the thousands, it came down to Charlie and some lady. We were way in the back, and she was sitting up front, so we didn't see who she was. Charlie wouldn't give up, and finally the lady backed down, and Charlie had his jersey. He got his picture with Sammy that showed up in the papers the next day. Most important was Charlie's generous gift to a worthy cause. (By the way; I think the lady was Mrs. Coors).

—Mary R.

**Meeting Sammy Sosa**

*Hi this is Aaron G. I was writing to say what I remember about you. I remember how you came to one of my parents' parties and you and I played Rush 2 (the racing game.) and you picked the hippie van as your vehicle. And you seemed to crash and burn up your car instead of race it. But one of the most recent memories was when I was at my parents' work and you were telling my mom about how when you were in Cleveland and you were being searched so many times. And most of them are because it seems the people working that day at the airport were either paranoid or stupid. But Charlie, you want to know something, I know we don't know each other as well as my parents do, but you and your family are the coolest family that I know. And you know what else, you are a strong person and I know you can and will pull through this. So I am sorry that this happened in the first place, but bud I can't wait to see you again soon, and best of luck, and I'm praying for you.*

*Signed your little friend, Aaron*

But maybe the best example of Charlie in action was the Advanced Project Management Training held in Washington D.C. During that busy week Charlie was simultaneously dealing with negotiating a settlement and getting the training done. It was the last week in October 2000. The cell phone was going almost non-stop, but Charlie was always working the case study problem to ensure his team's solutions to the project's problems was the most thorough. His competitive nature simply would not tolerate 2$^{nd}$ place (despite all the training staff's urging that there was no grading and no "right answer"). Not surprisingly, Charlie's team had the best Cost and Schedule Performance Index by week's end.

Life may bring challenges to us, but few can expect the intensity of response that Charlie Wolf brings. Give 'em hell, Charlie. We can't wait to have you back - providing more Charlie stories.

—Dick R.


*Hi Charlie,*

*My thoughts and prayers are with you. I was shocked to hear the news and pray that the surgery and recovery go well. You have always been an inspiration and I appreciate all you did for me in B771. Your confidence in me has made me a better person in my work activities today.*

*It seem like only yesterday (actually just a few months) since we were playing golf, drinking beer, and gambling at Mesquite. I enjoyed watching you play roulette, with all those chips in front of you. I remember a few years ago on our trip to Mesquite how you creatively played the 4th hole at the Palms. You may not even remember the specific details but they go something like this. Greg M. and I were playing with you and Kathy. This hole is a par 5 with an island surrounded by water along the right fairway. You hit a long tee shot but sliced it, and your golf ball landed right on the island. You had to go down another fairway to even get on the island. Needless to say, you made a few more great shots from there and ended up with a birdie on the hole. One of the all time great birdies in Mesquite history.*

*Anyway, hope these moments help put a smile on your face. You will continue to be in my thoughts and prayers. I'll be in touch soon.*

*Steve R.*


I do remember one time in high school that we were all going to Grandma & Grandpa Szabo's house and your dad didn't want to go because he wanted to play football with his friends. Grandma told him no at least two or three times because she didn't want him to get hurt while she was gone and finally she let him go play and no sooner did we get to grandma's house and she got a phone call that he got hurt and his teeth went right through his bottom lip. He had stitches inside and out.

Also I remember he went to Daytona Beach for spring break in a brown Maverick he had just bought but they didn't have any money to go. They slept in the car the whole time.

Hope all is well, love you
Aunt Pattie

*"The Equalizer"*

*Upon arriving at Rocky Flats, Charlie was assigned to Building 771, with Scott S. as his Deputy. Although Scott was one-and-a-half feet taller that Charlie, they were on an even plane when it came to character, leadership, and energy. Charlie received the energy level of a man 10 feet tall, and ran circles around all of us. Regardless of the person Charlie deals with (Congressman, Senator, President, etc.) he always rises to the occasion and comes out smelling like a rose. This is a quality I am still trying to master and emulate.*

*Thanks, David D.*

I recall a story about you, Charlie, that dealt (no pun intended) with a poker game at your house. One Friday evening after a hard day of restart, Dave M., Bill S., you and Doug Y. got together for a game of poker. It was dealer's choice and as the evening progressed the dealer selected the game in which each player is dealt two cards and the player bets on whether or not the next card they are dealt falls between the two cards they were initially dealt. Charlie, I was told you were dealt a three and a jack. You be the pot that your next card would fall between your two cards. The dealer, who I am told may have rigged the stack, dealt you a king. Doug went on to win the pot and you wrote Doug and IOU, signed H.C. Wolf. We now know the reason you didn't have ample cash on hand was due to the fact that you invested all Kathy's money as well as some of your own. Doug proudly displayed the IOU on his bulletin board for your entire tenure as the Facility Manager and to this day Doug still has that IOU. In fact, know how successful you have been in business (Corporate Director) as well as in you investments (written about in the Wall Street Journal), the IOU means even more to Doug. Was Doug the dealer?

Richard B.


CHARLIE, WE WANT YOU TO KICK ASS!!!!! IF ANYONE CAN BEAT IT, YOU ARE THE ONE!!!!

YOU WEREN'T THE FASTEST GUY AT OHIO STATE FOR ANY REASON! YOU WILL OUTRUN THIS TOO!!!

MY FAMILY IS THINKING OF YOU AND YOUR FAMILY. IF THERE IS ANYTHING WE CAN DO, PLEASE DO NOT HESITATE TO ASK.

GOD BLESS,
DANVE, KELLY, KYLE, RYAN & ADAM T.


*Amber, no stories, but I do want to provide a note. Your dad was such an inspiration in Building 771 at Rocky Flats. He infused the task with great energy, always positive in the face of huge tasks and grumpy people, and he turned a deflated and unhappy workforce into a proud, competent team. I always liked standing in his office, looking at the collage of pictures of him with the family – they created an impression of a strong, upbeat solid family man with a playful side, as sense of humor that laced his leadership at work as well. He was competent, genuine and personable to work with.*

*Along with every person who knows you dad, I wish him the very best fighting through this rough time.*

*George M.*


        Polly and I are so very concerned for Charlie, Kathy, and all of your family. Here's a Charlie Story. Hope it helps.
        I remember once years ago when I went by Charlie and Kathy Wolf's (maybe to pick up Kathy for work, I can't remember), I asked Charlie where he was working. He said FB-Line. I asked him why he was working there because it was a bit of a problem back then. Charlie said, "I want to work there. I asked to be assigned there". I said why in this world would you want to be assigned to FB-Line. Charlie's reply, as I later found out, was typical of the kind of man he is. He said, "I asked management what the toughest assignment was on the site. I told them I wanted the toughest assignment and that I was up to the challenge. Management said the toughest assignment was FB-Line and I told them that was what I wanted."

Sonny G.


    The above letters were a sample of what I received from my friends and family for my recovery book. I wanted to enclose some of the information to give folks an idea of how well these e-mails, calls, and letters help people. Most people are used to a short illness or disease. In those cases people go to the hospital and visit or call once. They do not realize that a brain tumor causes a long disability and, in a lot of cases, one may never recover.

When I was in the hospital for my first surgery, I got a giant signed card from the Denver office of the company I worked for. A couple of days later, I got a card from our corporate office in Boise. Both of them were great; they really helped me feel better knowing that they were thinking of me. But then I didn't hear from a number of people for quite a while. Kathy found out that they were worried that they might be bothering me, when actually the opposite was true.

I learned throughout that if you are open and honest about how you are suffering, it's amazing how people respond. A number of people are interested in what is happening to you and how you are doing. Most people know how to act when they are visiting someone in the hospital for a day or two. But when the illness lasts for a prolonged period of time, most people don't know how to react or what they can do. It's almost like you have to help them feel comfortable to help you.

I have been really lucky that in almost a year since my surgery, I am still getting support letters, e-mails, and phones calls from friends. In addition, I have lunch or dinner with friends a couple times a month. I don't know how long this will last, but it really shows the type of friends, relatives, and family you have.

To give back some of the support that I have received from my family and friends, I started volunteering at Children's Hospital in Denver, after getting my doctor's okay. I chose Children's in honor of my granddaughter. I volunteer for one morning a week and play with hospitalized children, some with problems worse than mine. I encourage people to volunteer at their local hospital. When I was working, I donated to various charities but didn't really have time to volunteer. I have found out that volunteering is a truly rewarding experience. Take advantage of the "free" time that you have away from work.

# Chapter
## 6

# *Treatment is not*
# *a Straight Line*

As I have already discovered from my long path from my initial surgery on July 1, 2002 until now, I understand that treatment will not follow a straight line.

On August 6$^{th}$, I had my first radiation session!! The treatment had begun. I was so excited to finally start treatment it was unbelievable. I would be treated using Intensity Modulation Radiation Therapy (IMRT) on a linear accelerator. Very cool stuff. The IMRT allows the radiation beams to be sent to the areas requiring treatment and to stay away from good brain tissue.

As an engineer, I thought the radiation treatment was really cool and would really like to study it. It would be really neat, if it weren't being done on me. Since it was, I needed to study how it worked. It was even more important because it was my life! I wanted to be sure I knew what was going on.

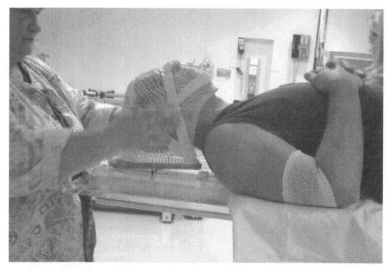

**Preparing for Radiation Therapy**

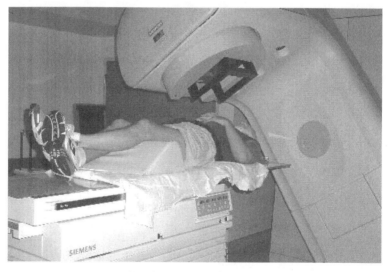

**The Linear Accelerator**

August 7th was my second radiation therapy. This is when I took the pictures of the table and my mask while I laid on the table. The doctor said that 6 beams were positioned on my brain while I was on the table. He said I would get 180 centigrays, or 180 Rad, each time. They used centigrays, an international unit of measure for radiation dose. The total dose for the entire treatment would be about 6000 Rad. Because of my nuclear work, I knew that a 1000 Rad exposure at one time could kill you. The doctor explained how the fatigue would mount with each session. He also said my skin would get patchy and I would start losing my hair after three or so visits. I would have a treatment every weekday for 6½ weeks until I reached the final dose of 6000 Rad. That would involve about 33 sessions. The 33 days ended on my birthday; I thought that was a good sign.

The next day, I started chemo as well. I finally started the first chemo and was glad that all treatments had finally begun. I was now putting a full assault on my body. I was going to start with two different chemo agents. The chemo is supposed to support the radiation treatment by destroying the microscopic cells that are still present after the surgical removal of the gross tumor cells.

I took Camptosar® (also referred to as CPT-11 or Irinotecan) by IV. It took about 90 minutes to complete delivery. I also took Temodar® (temozolomide) pills at night for the next five nights. The Camptosar damages the tumor cells' DNA, thereby interfering with the cell growth. Camptosar is primarily used for colon cancer. Temodar was approved for use in 1999, making it the first new chemotherapy agent for this type of brain tumor approved in the United States in 20 years. It is a cytotoxic agent that prevents the replication of cells that divide rapidly, including those in tumors. It controls the growth of both normal and brain tumor cells. The advantage is that the brain tumor cells are growing quicker, so these cells are affected faster. You hope it kills the tumor faster than it kills you.

They really tried to keep the effects of the chemo under control. My nurse, Mary, put Kytril® and atropine in my IV to start the chemo. The Kytril is used to prevent nausea and the atropine was used to prevent sweats, cramps, and diarrhea. The atropine caused dry mouth, increased heart rate, and dilated my pupils. I needed to stop eating at least two hours before taking the Temodar pills to help prevent me from getting sick. Temodar could cause constipation and Camptosar could cause diarrhea. Great combination! Even with all the preventatives, I felt pretty pukey during chemo. I felt that way the whole time.

Mary described more precautions and when to call the doctor if problems arose. The other dangers were uncontrolled vomiting, and leg and arm swelling or pain, which could mean possible blood clots. Paying attention to these symptoms is very important. It isn't as easy as it seems to identify the problems. I have had similar symptoms many times and did not know if they were clots or not.

The chemo treatments can be very risky even to a healthy person, so the doctors are very active in monitoring my health. The doctors want to ensure that the chemo treatments help me and do not hurt me.

As the doctors have stated, there is no silver bullet and the treatment of a tumor is trying the best treatments available and if that doesn't work, they try something else. The current treatments I am taking are considered the best by my oncologist. You won't find anyone that will guarantee a solution or a cure, but you need to be sure that you are comfortable with your doctors.

On August 10$^{th}$, my sister, Sally, came back for a visit. I was so glad she decided to come again. We all went to Alan's sister's wedding. Alan is Amber's husband. We had a great time at the wedding and it was lots of fun. I was really glad to get out.

The next day, we went for a hike in a park near us. It was great to start walking again. It was hot, but we had a good time. We took Sally to the ESPN Zone later to play games. It was really nice to do some activities that took my mind off my condition. I still had a lot of depression at night, but things were going well now.

Sally took me to my August 12$^{th}$ radiation treatment and got to see all the equipment and how I had to go through the treatment. Later that night we played Hearts and had a great time.

During this time, I also continued to have speech therapy. The therapist did a complete analysis and stated that my right lip did not respond as well as the left. I just thought that I would talk like *Rocky Balboa*, only better. By August 13$^{th}$, I was starting to look pretty good. Dr. Arenson was reducing my Decadron a little. Although the Decadron has some useful properties, it also has some long-term side effects. So it is important to get off or lower your steroids as soon as possible.

I had not had any problems with radiation. However, after the August 14th session, I had a pretty bad headache. It was probably more from medication changes than the radiation.

On Thursday, August 15th, Taylor and Amber took me to radiation. They got to see and sign my radiation mask; it's like Patrick Roy's. Roy was hockey goalie for the Colorado Avalanche who had his kids sign his stick before important games.

After this session, my back was sore due to the position I needed to stay in. The radiation attendants informed me that on Thursdays I could get a massage. I got my first massage and it helped a lot. The nurses suggested that I sign up for a weekly massage. The massages were great and it helped me after that week.

On Friday, I visited Dr. Bartczak. My temperature was at 97.9°F and I was looking well. It looked like Labor Day would be the last day for the antibiotics. I was really looking forward to completing antibiotics because I was tired of carrying the pump around and having the PICC line as my permanent buddy.

I decided to start writing this book on August 20, 2002. I had been thinking about it for a while and I wanted to document what really happens to someone with a serious brain tumor. I had never written a book before, but I thought this would make dealing with the tumor easier for me. It also turned out to be great speech therapy.

On August 22nd I had some strange cravings, very similar to a pregnant woman. In this particular case I wanted watermelon. I ate half the watermelon immediately and the rest the next day. A mushroom craving came later when my hair began falling out. The mushroom craving continued and we stopped at Outback Steak House many times to satisfy this craving. Kathy read something later that mushrooms were good for your white blood cells and watermelon has a lot of magnesium. So, my body must have been telling me something.

The radiation tours continued. On August 23rd I took Amber, Alan, and Taylor back to see how my radiation treatment was done. They could see how the mask worked and what the equipment looked like. Afterwards, Amber, Alan, Taylor, and I went out for breakfast. I had started to lose my hair on this day.

We took a family ride to Aspen on August 25th to get me out of the house again. When we left the house we saw a hot air balloon taking off and then, a whole group of them. It is amazing how you really enjoy looking at things a little more than you had in the past. We stopped at a few places along the way and played near a river. We also stopped at the Old Independence ghost town near the Continental Divide. We then drove to Aspen for lunch and walked throughout the town. We all had a great time and it allowed me to forget my problems for a while.

Two days later, I had another chemo regimen. This was my 2$^{nd}$ chemo treatment. I was still on the two-drug regimen of Camptosar and Temodar.

September 2$^{nd}$, J.J., my friend, took me to radiation. My friend, Bill, had set up a list of people from my current and former work locations to take me to radiation. It was really great. It helped because Kathy could work and I could meet friends and associates again. I really appreciate what Bill did and the support and willingness of my friends to help. I enjoyed my morning drives and discussions with my friends. Many times I would trap them in the house so I would have someone to talk to and so I could keep up with work, in a lot of cases. Having company was great.

September 1$^{st}$ was the last day for the antibiotic. It was great to finally get out the PICC line. The PICC line was removed on Tuesday the 3$^{rd}$ in the doctor office. I didn't feel anything at all. It was great to be done with it. I was also pretty excited, my Granddaughter Taylor would no longer be afraid to hold my hand on that side.

I took Taylor to swim at the Highlands Ranch pool. It had a slide, whale, and other things. She really had a good time. It was about the last time it would be open and I had promised to take her swimming. I didn't know if I would be able to do this with her next year and wanted to get things done. I thought she would like to swim for about half an hour, but two and a half hours later, I had to essentially force her out of the pool.

On September 10$^{th}$ my oncologist allowed me to start getting off Decadron. I found out today that the new chemo drug BCNU could cause a number of problems. A virus, CMV, could infect bone marrow and cause immuno-suppression problems. They had to do a check of my system for the CMV virus. This could have affected the treatment protocol. CMV (cytomegalovirus) is an opportunistic infection and very common. About 85% of the U.S. population tests positive for CMV by the time they are 40 years old. This needed to be checked because of the problem of taking BCNU if you are infected with CMV. I was pretty concerned because I was to start the additional protocol using the BCNU. It was suppose to be one of the best and I did not want to reduce the effectiveness of my treatments.

On September 12th we went in to see Dr. Fullagar. He said that everything went well and that I just needed to get him a copy of the new MRI.

September 14th was Kathy's and my twenty-third anniversary. I had gotten pretty bad at keeping my journal up to speed, but I had been doing the girls' books at night. Kathy, Amber, Taylor and I went to the Rockies Game to celebrate our anniversary. We then went to the ESPN Zone for fun.

On September 17th, it was time for chemo number three. Chemo drugs are an important part of the cure but can cause various dangerous problems. The Camptosar burned a great deal this time as it entered my arm. It was very difficult to handle and it left burns in my veins. The pain stopped a few hours after the treatment.

As I was getting close to finishing my radiation treatments, I became pretty sleepy. The amount of radiation received had affected my alertness. As a result, I slept for several hours during each day. The radiation caused the fatigue.

Dr. Arenson stated that we would do the next MRI in 2 to 3 weeks. That was scary, because I would then find out what had happened to the tumor following my radiation therapy.

September 20, 2002. My birthday and my last day of radiation!! I was given my mask to keep and I proudly hung it on the wall at home with my name, like a trophy. I lived with that thing for 33 sessions and saw it as a true savior of my life. I mounted my mask and put the title for my book on the plaque: *Damn the Statistics, I Have a Life to Live*. Again, small victories are very important as you fight this disease and the mask represents a major victory for me.

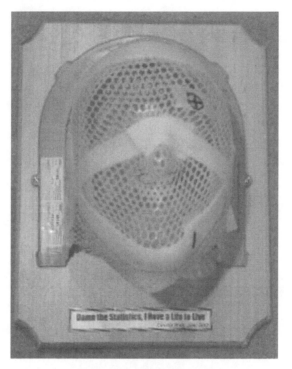

**Radiation Mask Plaque**

On September 24th, we stopped into the doctor's office and found out that we had a good result on the serum test. I had mono when I was little, but not CMV. I didn't even know that I had had mono. He also found out that I had a low white blood count and we were worried that it would postpone Kathy's and my trip to Yellowstone to celebrate the completion of radiation. The doctor gave me a shot of Neupogen® and Kathy would have to give me four more on our trip. The Neupogen was required to boost up the white blood cells and keep me from getting an infection.

Going to Yellowstone National Park provided some additional steps towards my goals. The first step was that I was finally getting out of the house to do something and the second was getting to see Yellowstone. Although things go well, each day you are never sure if you will survive much longer. Yellowstone was one place that I have always wanted to see.

**Yellowstone National Park**

Kathy and I had a great time. We walked through the park starting at about 7:00 a.m. each morning and continued on until 7:00 p.m. or later at night. We enjoyed the variety and number of geysers. It was great and unlike anything else I had ever seen. We saw buffalo, elk, and many other animals. The bull elks bugling at each other was neat. I had never really seen that before and it was a true treat. We had a great time and it gave me a brief vacation from my treatments.

MRI day! On October 2$^{nd}$ I had the first MRI since surgery. Dr. Arenson looked at the MRI and was very pleased that the results were positive. We were pretty happy that the first MRI came out well. We knew it could change, but it was great news! It gave hope that the radiation and chemo treatments were doing their jobs. Again, it allowed for more focus on the positive!

With the MRI over, we started the next chemo phase. That phase involved the addition of BCNU. BCNU has been known as the brain tumor chemotherapy agent of choice for over 20 years. It is able to cross the blood-brain barrier for treatment. This is important because a lot of drugs are unable to cross that barrier and provide help. The main reason BCNU is used is that it has been able to keep patients alive for 2 years longer than other protocols.

One of the main problems with BCNU is that it can cause lung damage. The lung toxicity from BCNU can be severe enough to cause death. In fact, BCNU has been known to cause death in patients in remission as well. Because of the effect that the BCNU could have on my lungs, a lung function test was performed to see if there could be any problems. I had some trouble with the test and it was performed twice. I had to blow hard into the tubes and the pressure really affected me. I had always scored above my age group average for breathing tests my whole life, but in this one, I was slightly below average.

After a successful day, the evening turned a little ugly. At 9:30 p.m., I was doing well and the phone rang. It was my daughter, Amber, wanting to hear about the good MRI news. All I could talk was gibberish. This was the same thing that happened when my first symptoms occurred. We went into panic mode. Kathy ran to get my Ativan®, thinking that maybe I was having a seizure, but I had already pulled some out of my wallet. My daughter thought I was teasing her at first, but she soon became scared as well. It was very difficult to handle this, especially after the positive MRI.

Kathy called Dr. Arenson's office and we headed to the Littleton ER. When we arrived, they took me straight back – again. They thought I might be having a stroke this time. That really scared me more because it was affecting my brain again. I had a CAT scan, some Decadron, 2 baby aspirin, and Neurontin at 900 mg. They wanted to reduce any potential for swelling.

It was ironic that the ER doctor I saw that night was the same doctor I saw on June 3$^{rd}$ when this all started! What are the odds? It was also impressive that the doctor remembered me and what had happened. He must have see hundreds of patients since the first visit, but I was a standout. There was no evidence of a stroke, and it didn't seem to be a seizure so I was deemed stable enough to go home, even though I couldn't talk.

The following day, October 3$^{rd}$, Kathy called Mary and Kassie to see what we should do. Dr. Arenson called at 12:30 p.m. and told me to take four baby aspirin. He believed that it was probably a motor problem, perhaps a small stroke, but not a seizure. They were going to need to do some tests. He set up a consultation with a neurologist that specialized in strokes and would admit me. I had to be admitted to the hospital – again. It seemed that there was always something wrong. I was still having speech problems at this time. The doctor's office, especially Mary, kept things a step ahead of me. Mary had scheduled everything before we arrived at the office.

I got an MRA to check arteries and a Carotid NIVA (sonogram). The Carotid NIVA (Non Invasive Vascular Assessment) was performed to check for blockages in the neck arteries. I saw a stroke specialist, to check to see if I had had a stroke. His initial belief was that the symptoms were caused by a temporary restriction in the blood vessels.

By that afternoon, they believed the blood vessels looked good. There may have been some fluid in the brain lining, which might have been signs of another infection so Dr. Bartczak was contacted. I was admitted and back on the 9th floor of Swedish Hospital again. I had no temperature, pulse was good, and blood pressure was excellent. No evidence of infection.

The next morning, I had an EEG at 8:00 a.m. to get a brain scan. I also received two more Decadron and a Pepsid to help my stomach. Dr. Arenson thought that perhaps my problems were related to a TEI, or a temporary restriction of the blood vessels. The electro-encephalographic (EEG) was used to check for evidence of a seizure.

Although they had taken blood samples, they still wanted a spinal tap. It was a little before noon when they did the spinal tap. I had a couple L-4 and L-5 back surgeries a few times in the early nineties, so I was not surprised when I had two lumbar punctures and they did not get the amount of sample they wanted, but what they obtained was sufficient.

The spinal fluid was ok, but Dr. Arenson left me in the hospital on my back so I would not get a spinal headache. Dr. Arenson thought it could have been a vascular constriction. The stroke doctor stopped by and really thought that it was irritation from the gadolinium contrast agent from the MRI. The EEG showed a little slowness on the left side but no signs of an ongoing seizure. So, there was no definitive answer. I only needed a baby aspirin a day as an anticoagulant.

We were lucky, this episode did not affect the next chemo treatment. So on October 8, we started chemo treatment number 4. This time it was a three-drug treatment. I was on BCNU, Temodar, and Camptosar. The Camptosar burned my arm like crazy again. We would later find out I had a problem with Camptosar, but this time it was just the pain.

On October 13, 2002 we headed over to Amber's to take Taylor out to ride a horse. They had a secret for us that Amber was expecting another baby in May. This made things tough when I thought of how much I might not be able to share with this new grandchild. It also gave me more determination to push ahead.

**With Granddaughter Taylor**

On October 22, 2002, it seemed like things were going well. I received my flu shot, and was given Neupogen to get my white blood count back up. It had dropped because of the chemo. I also requested and got approval to drive in the neighborhood but was told to stay off highways and avoid night driving. This was another major milestone! Things were going so well that I wanted to get back to work.

# *Chapter*
## 7

# *The Problems with the Brain are as Large as the Tumor*

Language, reading and memory are what separates us from the animals and makes us who we really are. But what happens if one day you are unable to communicate? This chapter will take you through the experiences I went through, when I was unable to read or speak! There are many different names for the language problems caused on this side of the brain. The most common is aphasia. Aphasia is the loss or breakdown of the ability to make sense of language. It does not affect a person's intelligence, but makes them seem like they are in a foreign country. They may not understand what is being stated, but they are just as intelligent as before.

Dr. Fullagar had agreed to do my operation on July 1, 2002. My tumor is on the left temporal parietal lesion, which really worried me because of the potential effects it will continue to have with my brain. Worrying about what will happen to my brain functions during my biopsy and other events was very scary. Before brain surgery, besides asking a lot of questions of your doctor, be sure you do research on not only the operation, but also what you may expect in terms of your brain functions. That will also help you come up with the questions to ask your doctor.

The day after my biopsy on June 11, 2002, my mental capacity was pretty good. I had some trouble with concentration and focus, but in general all functions were only affected slightly. I had some right leg problems, but they went away quickly. This was really the first time that I realized I might have cognitive problems.

On June 28th, as surgery time came closer I was even more nervous and wanted to get the surgery over with. I didn't know what would happen and how to prepare until after the surgery. The surgery was the key to my recovery or lack there of. Kathy and Stephanie took me to dinner and then we rented the movie, *A Beautiful Mind*. As I said before, I really enjoyed the movie and had tears as I watched it understanding that he had problems, some similar to the minor ones I had with my brain. As I watched that movie, I had the strange thought that it was a good thing that this was happening to me, because someone else might not be able to endure it.

I had my surgery on July 1st, and after my surgery, I was unable to read and speak. My family showed me pictures to help me communicate without speaking, but I was unable to identify many of the pictures. Remember, the most difficult part is that your intelligence is not affected, but things don't make sense to you.

The type of aphasia that I had was called global aphasia. It was a result of severe damage to language areas of the brain. I had lost all language functions including speech and understanding language. I could not read, write, or understand language.

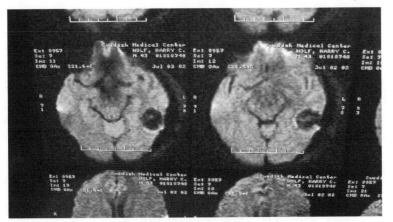

**Hole Left in Brain**

I was glad I wrote a note to my family and friends just in case I couldn't speak after surgery. But what I should have written was a second letter to discuss what I wanted done if I couldn't speak or read or if I experienced other mental function problems.

Since I was unable to speak or read, I was extremely frustrated. It was one of the most frustrating points of my life. I could not recognize my own name or even recognize photos of my family.

Another item that I noticed was that I had no modesty when I couldn't speak and read. I don't understand why it worked that way, but as long as I couldn't speak, my modesty didn't exist. This is a great point to make sure your family and friends are aware of. My daughters saw much more than they desired. If I had to go to the bathroom, I just flipped up my gown and went!

I was very clumsy as well. I was trying to take my medicine and spilled it almost every time. One time I spilled it all over my bed and tried to say, "God damn it." It didn't come out right, but my daughters understood it.

The morning of July 4, 2002, I still was not talking, but my motor skills appeared better. That afternoon, I started talking. It was coming back in pieces. I let my family know that I had a headache and wanted to know what time it was. It was 3:30 in the afternoon. I then wanted to know who was in the room. It was one of my doctors.

My mother called and I was able to talk a little and was able to mention that Stephanie was a smart ass. As my memory started to come back little by little, a lot of things were pretty interesting. I told

Amber, my oldest, that I remembered her little girl (Taylor) and that I remembered the awake craniotomy. I then said, "I saw my brain and it scared me to death." Talking was getting better every minute and as I got up to go to the bathroom, my modesty had returned.

On July 5th, I was able to speak even better, but completely unable to read and had a great deal of cognitive issues and memory. An example was when I was calling Kathy at 4:00 p.m. that afternoon, I called her, "George," "Hanna," "Anna," "Alan," "Tammy," and then finally "Kathy."

A lot of my speech problems were associated with similar things. When asked who the president was, I said, "Ford," "Nixon," "Clinton," and then "Bush." I also had a lot of similar problems with names, etc. I had the most problems with my daughter, Stephanie. Since I remembered my sister Sally when she was as young as my daughter and my granddaughter, Taylor, I often called Stephanie either Sally or Taylor.

I had a great deal of swelling after surgery and the doctors and speech therapists stated I wouldn't improve until the swelling went down. My head was huge.

I could not read at all! I could not even recognize my name when I saw it. It was really frustrating. I could not understand a single thing. The worst part was that I could not learn something if someone told me what it was because the wiring of my brain didn't work that way. It was not that I didn't know it – it was just that the input/output signals were messed up.

My mom tried to help by working with some colored dice with me. She would have me pick up three dice, red, blue, and yellow. I would pick up red, blue, and yellow. She then asked what I had in my hand. I could not tell her. Even though I just picked them up, I could not identify them. She could ask me to pick up one color such as yellow. I could pick up the yellow, but could not say yellow when she asked. It was very frustrating and very difficult to explain that to people. My family would also take me through children's books that had pictures with simple words. I could not recognize the words. If I did get one, a little later I could not recognize the same word again. Talk about frustration.

They could teach a child to read much easier. Just remember, it's more like reading a foreign language than a schoolbook. I finally gave up trying because I could not make any steps forward. I would try to read things every once in a while to see if I had improved, but I had not. Another frustration was with the insurance requirements for the company, I could not get speech therapy set up in a timely manner, and I really needed it. I was sleeping only two hours a night and I was extremely frustrated with my language and speech issues.

On Thursday, July 18th, I was admitted to the hospital due to swelling in my head from an infection in the wound area on my head. The pain was incredible. On Sunday morning, I had my second craniotomy to clean up the infection. My head was now a lot smaller since the second craniotomy was able to get the infection cleaned up. I was still unable to read and had a lot of memory issues, but I didn't lose my speech this time.

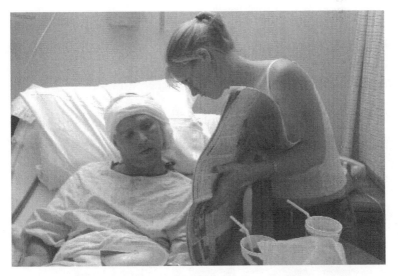

**Stephanie Helping Me Identify Pictures in Newspaper**

I was still frustrated at being unable to read, but I was feeling a lot better after this surgery. On July 25th, as I was lying in the bed, I looked at the windowsill and saw a Crunch 'n Munch® box. The key thing was I could read it! The Crunch 'n Munch box was the first thing I could read. I had tears coming down my face and was repeating over and over, "I can read!!" I had to call Kathy at home, even though it was late at night, to tell her. I really had more confidence now; it was the first sign of improvement. Kathy would tell everyone later that my epiphany was a Crunch 'n Munch box!

I was really unable to read until July 27th and unable to fully describe what happened around surgery and the days after. Don't get me wrong; my reading didn't improve dramatically. I was only able to read one or two words at a time.

I have confidence that I will eventually make it through all the reading issues so that I can do whatever I want. It is just a different type of learning. I have made it through several potential fatal events already, so I should be able to handle this. I had a seizure that could have killed me, that was followed by a biopsy, then my awake craniotomy, followed by an infection in my head, and a second craniotomy to remove the infection. Knowing that I made it through these events so far has kept me going.

On July 28, 2002, I could read a little and played my first game in the hospital with Stephanie. We played Scrabble and cards. I really enjoyed having the ability to function a little normally. I had not been able to do activities like this since before my first surgery.

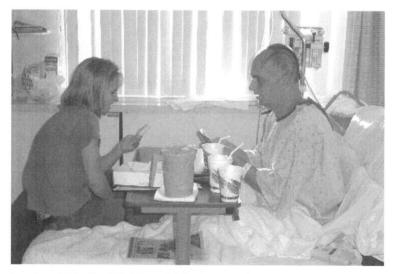

**Playing My First Game Following Surgery**

Over the next couple of weeks, my reading and memory improved as I went through my problems with aphasia. Phonemic paraphasia is one of the problems I still have. As time goes by, I also improve, but it is not easy. Phonemic paraphasia is where I substitute, add, or rearrange letter sounds so that the word that comes out has a similar sound to the word I am trying to say.

When I first entered the hospital I was diagnosed with the symptoms of neologism (using made up words) and phonemic paraphasia. At least that's what I heard from the therapists. The therapists started me with very simple tasks such as looking at a picture and identifying the object, action, or color. Colors, numbers, dates, and time are four areas that are still problematic. For example, I seem to switch orders of magnitude with numbers: saying "five hundred" when I mean "fifty."

I have been working on improving my aphasia the best I can. I continue to work, but I get very frustrated because I am not making much progress. I often have a great deal of trouble finding the right word. I have it in my head most of the time, but just can't get it out. In most cases, it takes me about five to six seconds to get the word I want to say out. I understand everything that is told to me; it is just the damage to my brain that doesn't allow me to make the point I want.

Reading is still very difficult. I cannot read words very quickly, if I can read them at all. I can no longer scan something and understand generally what it says. I need to read every word, like in elementary school. My speech therapist said that I am reading at about a fifth or sixth grade level.

I am extremely grateful that I am able to function a pretty normal life, despite my problems. I will probably never be able to use my chemical engineering degree or my MBA in the manner I want, but I still have all my brainpower. I am also extremely frustrated that I may not be able to do the job I enjoy the most – Project Management. The aphasia will probably prevent me from being able to complete all of my life goals.

The doctors have said that the radiation will continue to affect me years later. The chemotherapy is also continuing to have an impact on the tumor location. After my body is able to recover from these onslaughts, I'm hopeful that I'll gain more reading and speaking skills.

# Chapter
# 8

# *Damn the Statistics,*
# *I Have a Life to Live!*

I wasn't going to let the statistics get me; I had things to do. I planned on getting back to work after I met the criteria that I thought would work. I had a goal that after I finished radiation treatment, did well on the follow-up MRI, and did well through the first chemo with the BCNU, I would try to go back to work.

I also needed to see how well I could do with the aphasia problems and if the reading problems would be too great. The aphasia did not affect my intelligence, even though speech was sometimes jumbled and I had trouble remembering words on a regular basis. The final tests were to fly to Boise by myself and talk to my bosses to see if they would be up to me returning to work.

On October 16, 2002, I flew to Boise to receive my Eagle Award. The Eagle Award is a company award nominated by peers and then evaluated by a management team as to who the winners will be. I was awarded the Mentoring Employee Development Excellence

Award from the corporate side; this was the most important award I could receive since it was for helping other employees. The Company Operating Officer and President were there. After receiving the award, I had time to talk to my management team and they stated that they would be glad to see me back. With this basis, I made the request of returning to work to Dr. Arenson.

On October 22$^{nd}$, after a conversation with the doctor, he wrote a note that approved my return to work. He wasn't real excited about letting me go back to work and even had a major discussion on how it usually didn't work because of the chemo, the fatigue, and other reasons. But, I still wanted to take the chance and see what I could and couldn't do.

It was great going back, because the first event in late October was the Leadership Conference for the company. With that I was able to meet everyone again and get an update on where the company had gone while I was absent. This was in Boise and the spouses were invited, which worked out really well because Kathy could keep an eye on me during the trip.

I returned to the office the next week. I had a meeting with the office manager, who was also setting up some help for me. I really didn't want help, I wanted to do it myself, but I knew this was probably the best. That way in case I had more problems, the company would have a backup. It felt good getting back to work. I spent the first week getting up to speed and finding out where things stood since I had been out for almost 6 months.

Work was very difficult. I really had a hard time with the reading and comprehension aspects of the job. I used verbal communications to compensate for the reading troubles.

November 5$^{th}$ was chemo treatment number five. I used Camptosar, Temodar and Taxol® was added for the first time. The Taxol was added to replace the BCNU since there had been some problems with the BCNU in the protocol, so this was thought to be a good substitute and safer.

The next day Kathy and I headed to South Carolina to help at the Savannah River Site. I didn't think that this trip would be too bad, but it was the start of the end of my work try. We really didn't expect any additional problems and the Taxol was supposed to be easier than the BCNU treatment. I had been tolerating the chemo treatments fairly well. Unfortunately things did not start out very well.

While in South Carolina, I didn't feel well by about the third day. My blood counts must have started dropping based on what we found out later. The Camptosar really made me sick. I started with some mild diarrhea on the trip, and a couple Imodium® would have kept things under control. I didn't follow the doctor's orders very well, he said to keep diarrhea under control when it started. I should have kept taking the Imodium.

The Taxol also caused a great deal of muscle pain. The nurse had told me to take L-Glutamine powder in large doses to help. It helped some, but I was in great pain for about four days. This trip was starting to be really tough between the pain and the diarrhea.

I then went from South Carolina to Cleveland on Monday without Kathy. I attended a course on Tuesday, November 12th, and went to a meeting on Wednesday. I was in real trouble. I had had very bad diarrhea for a couple days.

I finally broke down and called the doctor's office. I talked to Dr. Arenson who told me to take two doses of Imodium now and two more in an hour and then one dose every hour until the diarrhea had stopped for four hours. It was terrible; because my diarrhea was so bad I could not fly back home until the next day. I wouldn't have been able to last on the plane.

I finally got a plane back home on the afternoon of Thursday, November 14th. I really didn't let anyone know how bad this was. It seemed that I was suffering another setback.

The plane trip was tough and I got a ride back from the airport from my assistant. I didn't give her a clue on how bad I was. I arrived at home just before 8:00 p.m. and called the doctor. The doctor told me to go to the hospital to get hydrated. That's when the problems started again.

By 8:50 p.m. I had a fever of 101.4°F and knew that I was staying. As a chemo patient, any fever lands you in the hospital. It's good for you and should keep you safe, but once you get in the hospital, it's tough to get out! The ER doctor was very thorough and started various tests to eliminate some problems. I had stool and blood samples, and a chest x-ray.

The hospital was full, so I had to stay in the emergency room until 3:30 in the morning. By that time, my white blood count results had come back very low and I was quarantined in the room so that I could avoid exposure to potential infections. They administered Neupogen and started me on antibiotics. My fever was still 101°.

I was transferred to the temporary holding floor. It was great, I would be on the private floor to keep me from infection and have no problems. Unfortunately, I had the worst nurse I had ever met. Since I had spent so many days in the hospital, I knew which nurses were good and she was absolutely the worst. I still had diarrhea and couldn't get the nurse to do anything. I requested my Neurontin first thing in the morning and she still hadn't brought it to me by noon. She said the pharmacy was slow. (The ER guys had gotten it in a few minutes.) I won't go into any more complaining, but when doctor Arenson arrived, we worked on getting to the seventh floor as soon as possible.

However, the nurse wanted to keep me for her shift and delayed my move. The last straw was when she said she would delay my food delivery to the other room so I could stay there longer. I said, "I want out now!"

Dr. Arenson gave me Famvir® for a cold sore and opium tincture for the diarrhea. The diarrhea was a still going pretty strong.

By Saturday the 16th, I was feeling pretty good and I did not seem to have an infection. I no longer had any temperature and was ready to get out. Besides, the Ohio State Football game was not on the TV in the hospital. My white blood count was doing well and therefore I wanted to get out. Both doctors filling in for the weekend agreed I could get out.

When I saw Dr. Arenson on Tuesday, he wasn't too happy that I had gotten out of the hospital before my diarrhea had completely stopped. He gave me more opium tincture for the diarrhea. It still took two more days until my diarrhea stopped. The doctor stated that we were getting pretty close to not being able to use the Camptosar anymore.

When I went to the doctor on November 25th, I was met by Pam, the Patient Care Coordinator, and was essentially ambushed by the doctors and nurses, and told that I could not work anymore. It was pretty devastating, as I had put a lot of pressure on myself to be able to work. I also put a lot a pressure on myself to show others, and myself, that I could return.

However, the doctors and nurses really had my benefit in mind. They wanted to be sure I survived this terrible disease and that I needed to spend time working on my health. I also realized that my current cognitive situation needed to be worked on before I could return as well. It was a really tough week, because I had to leave work and go back on disability. I spent the next day turning work over to another person, and then headed home for Thanksgiving.

My next MRI was conducted on December 10, 2002. It started out pretty typical. They could not find veins, as usual, and it took three tries to get the IV in. We then went for my chemo.

Then we met with Dr. Arenson. In general, everything looked good and it even looked like the tumor was shrinking. However, there were a couple of areas that had cholene spikes. The cholene is indicative of abnormal tissue such as tumor. The one spot was in the area of the original tumor. The doctor needed to get more information from the radiologist to see if it was a problem.

Since I had problems with the Camptosar, I just got Taxol and Temodar during chemo. Talking to the doctor, the MRI was not all clear as we had expected. I found out by phone on Friday and just cried after I heard the news. We had just had chemo, so there was not really much else to do for now. We would find out more on Tuesday. This was a real blow. It was the first time that it looked like the tumor might be coming back.

To top things off on the weekend, I was working in the garage when the ladder I was on broke. I fell and broke my left wrist at about 6:30 p.m. Sunday evening. That was about all Kathy could take. She was very worried about me as it was. I had problems on the MRI, and then I broke my arm. Now she was worried that the broken arm might delay my next chemo treatment. She is a very strong woman, but this was very tough for her to handle.

On December 17th we met with Dr. Arenson. He stated that the scan was confusing and we would probably not know what the issue was until the next MRI. We would start back with BCNU because it was more aggressive, and because I could take Camptosar at a lower dosage. He also mentioned that we would add biological therapy such as thalidomide, tamoxiphen, or Celebrex®. I didn't really understand how these worked. I know these drugs are not intended to cure the tumor, but just keep it from growing any further.

I was staying up late again since the latest findings. Staying up late and getting up early seems to give you the feeling of being in more control and having more time. The findings brought more depression and I cried more each night. But again, I was determined to defeat this. I was determined to win the war.

I received my second BCNU treatment on February 4, 2003, following another MRI with the same questionable spots. The treatment involved Camptosar, BCNU, and Temodar. This one was a little scarier because the BCNU had caused fatalities as a result of lung damage. I needed it to help survive, but was worried.

The entire CNI team got together on Friday, February 7th, to review my MRIs. The good news was that they didn't think that the tumor was coming back. The bad news was they thought that the abnormal readings were due to a small stroke. I must have had a stroke after all back in October when I had the speech problems.

On February 25, 2003, I had surgery again. This time I had surgery to have a port installed into my upper chest. The port is similar to the PICC line except that it is fully contained in my chest. This was required because the veins in my arms had been completely destroyed as a result of constantly being poked by needles. My nurse had suggested the port a while ago, but I had resisted another surgery. The port was placed under my skin to be used for blood draws, chemo, and so forth. It was placed under my chest on the left side and a catheter was then inserted into the vena cava vessel at the entrance of the right atrium of the heart. It sounds kind of scary, but so far it has been great for me. The surgeon installed the port in about one-hour in the hospital out patient area. The port does not require all the extra work and maintenance that other pieces of equipment do. A special needle that looks like a fishhook is used to enter the port. I have a dual lumen port, which means it has two sides to work. I now wish I had done it sooner.

On March 4, 2003, I had bad nosebleeds and had very low platelets and required a transfusion. This was the first use of my port other than blood draws.

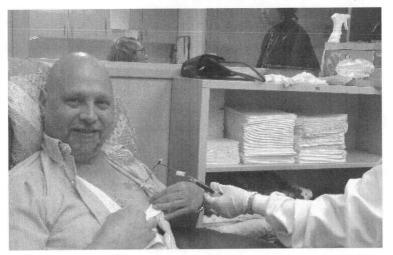

**Using the Port**

We had prepared to take a vacation the first week in April 2003 since I hadn't had one for a long time. We had tickets to the practice rounds of the Masters Golf tournament and had been looking forward to it for a while. We weren't sure if we were going to make it, since I hadn't been doing so well with my chemotherapy treatments.

We had my blood measured the week before and my white cells were very low and my readings were just lines on the chart (below detectable). The nurse got to work and I had an injection to raise my white cells and an injection to raise my red blood cells. I had already had a platelet transfusion about two weeks earlier.

It was now Tuesday, April 1st, and my blood readings showed that my white blood cells had done real well since the injection and in fact were the best I ever had. After another injection to boost my red cell count, the nurse said I was ready to go on my vacation.

On Wednesday we headed to my daughter Amber's house, and she took us to the airport. We didn't have any problems and were in Atlanta that afternoon. We had enough time to go to downtown Atlanta and go through the shops and just relax.

The next morning we headed to Hilton Head Island for a couple of days. When we got there, it was in the 70's and we were able to walk on the beach. It was a little windy, and it was a little cool. But we enjoyed a nice walk on the beach. Saturday, April 5th, was a really nice day. The temperature was in the 70's and there was very little breeze. It was great. We lazed around the pool. We had taken a nice walk around the beach and Kathy got pretty sunburned.

The next morning, we headed to the Masters practice rounds in Augusta, Georgia. We stayed with our friends, John and Margaret, while we went to the practice rounds. We had a great time with John and Margaret. However, it was cold and raining and the Monday practice rounds were cancelled. We tried again on Tuesday and had better luck. We got to see the golfers we wanted to see. I was excited to see Tiger Woods, as I had not seen him play. We sat on the 10th green and really had fun, even with the rain.

The next day we went to the Par 3 Tournament. We had a good time and found a seat between the 8th and 9th green. We got there at the start and had a chance to see all the golfers we wanted. It was especially cool to see Arnold Palmer, Jack Nicolas, and Gary Player playing together. The 9th hole was especially great as Jack and Gary put their shots within a foot and Arnold was about 19 feet away. He sunk his and the crowd went wild. Then Gary and Jack sunk their putts for all three to birdie. We had seen all the golfers we wanted and Kathy suggested we leave. As we headed out, it started to pour again.

**At the 2003 Masters**

94

On May 2, 2003, Amber gave me a second grandbaby. Adam David Cain was born at 10:21 p.m. We were all happy and he was really cute. Taylor stayed over at our house the first night and with her parents at the hospital on the second night. The following week, Kathy was on a business trip and the kids were keeping me company. I ended up in the doctor's office with a very bad nosebleed and had to have the doctors cauterize the area to stop the bleeding.

Charlotte stayed with me on Monday night, May 5th, and took me to the doctor the next day. Later that afternoon we played pool and had a great time. Stephanie was next on the list as my help. We went to dinner and then on Wednesday morning set up a checking and a credit card account for her as well. I then went to Amber's to stay the night and visit with the baby. I had a great time and stayed until after 3 p.m. before going home.

May 22, 2003 was Stephanie's high school graduation. I almost didn't make it at first. I had a bad case of diarrhea as a result of my chemo treatment. I took the appropriate medication and was ready by the time graduation started. We had a pretty good group of family members for graduation. My mom was there, Kathy's parents were there, my brother and two of his kids came, and Stephanie's sisters were there. It was a good day and a great time. I wasn't sure I was going to see her graduation when I first got my tumor, so I met another one of my goals.

As the end of May approached, I was coming up on one year since my tumor problems began. It was ironic that my short-term disability ended on May 27 and I began long-term disability on May 28th. This was one of my worst days. I was no longer employed and even worse, I no longer worked for Washington Group International, the company that had been great to my family and me. I plan on going back as soon as I can, if I can.

On Sunday, June 1, I went fly fishing for the first time in my life. I went with a group called Reel Recovery. It is a new group formed for men with brain tumors. We were the first group to go. I was starting to feel pretty good, as I was back to fishing again. It was a wonderful weekend and all the men attending had a great time. It was a little funny as I caught the first fish, a blue gill. There weren't supposed to be any blue gills in that Colorado pond, but it was pretty cool for our group to have caught one. That night I had time to talk with other brain tumor men and the leaders for the group. We built some very good friendships.

On June 2$^{nd}$, we had a fly-fishing lesson and instruction on the different kinds of flies. That day was a lot of fun and I actually learned how to fly fish. I even caught a few trout as well.

June 3, 2003, what else can I say? It was exactly one year since I had my seizure. The guys gave me a good cheer and they really understood how much it meant. One thing that brought us back to reality was that one of the members of our group had a tumor return after a couple of clear years and needed surgery. We wished him well and he had all of us realizing how we must live with this disease and how it can always return.

Once 9:30 a.m. passed, I felt better that I did not have another seizure. That night, I again stayed up late, thrilled I was still alive, but at the same time I fought off the tears because my body was a mess from the chemo and I still had months of treatment to go. I am also tired of being tired all the time. Between that and the medication and chemo, it is very tough each day. I saw an *ER* show where one of the guys gave up on his chemo and on his life. I would never give up, but can understand his thoughts. I am going to beat this disease, but as I fight, I know my life is shorter that it was before, I don't know how much shorter, but even when I think I am ahead, it may come back at anytime. It's tough to face death every day of your life.

I now have made it through one year as a survivor. I didn't think I would make it when it first happened, but I am still here on June 3, 2003. My friends, family, coworkers, and medical professionals are the real reason I am still here. I look forward to extending my life further and defeating this disease.

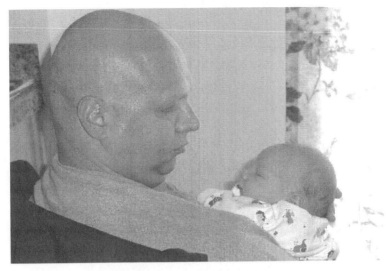

**With New Grandson, Adam**


On Thursday, June 11, 2003, I will have my next MRI to find out how I am doing. Since this book was designed to cover my first year, you will need to wait for my second book to see how year two went!

# *About the Author*

H. Charles Wolf is a husband, father, grandfather, former nuclear facility manager, and a brain tumor victim. He has worked in America's most dangerous facility, as dubbed by Peter Jennings. He has been on the front page of the *Wall Street Journal*. His education includes a chemical engineering degree from the Ohio State University and an MBA from the University of South Carolina. He continues to struggle with the aphasia caused by the tumor surgery. Writing this book was great therapy.

Made in the USA
San Bernardino, CA
05 September 2013